Internal Body Mechanics for Tai Chi, Xingyi and Bagua

How to Build a Foundation of Skill in the Internal Chinese Martial Arts Without the Mystical Mumbo Jumbo

Ken Gullette

Photography by Nancy Gullette

FIRST EDITION – July, 2018

Published by Internal Fighting Arts, LLC

Copyright © 2018 Internal Fighting Arts, LLC

All rights reserved.

ISBN-10: 0692112669
ISBN-13: 978-0692112663

DEDICATION

This book…..oh, who am I kidding? It isn't just this book! None of my teaching activities during the past 15 years would have been possible without the love and support of my wife, Nancy Gullette.

CONTENTS

	Acknowledgments	i
1	The Six Key Body Mechanics	1
2	The Centered Stance and the Ground Path	14
3	Maintaining Peng Jin	34
4	Internal Movement and the Kua	50
5	Dan-Tien Rotation	65
6	Manipulating Peng and Whole-body Movement	82
7	Silk-Reeling Energy	100
8	Where Do You Go From Here?	174
9	About the Author	179

Instructional DVDs by Ken Gullette

Internal Strength DVDs
** Internal Strength for Tai Chi, Hsing-I and Bagua
** Silk-Reeling Energy

Chen Taiji DVDs
** Chen 19 Form
** Chen 38 Form
** Chen Laojia Yilu Form
** Tai Chi Fighting Applications (3-DVD Set)
** Chen Broadsword Form
** Chen Straight Sword Form
** Chen Straight Sword Form Applications
** Chen Pear Blossom Spear Form
** Push Hands
** Close-Up Self-Defense with Tai Chi "Energies" and Methods
** 7 Internal Fighting Strategies

Xingyiquan DVDs
** Five Fist Postures
** Fighting Applications of the Five Fist Postures
** Five Element Linking Form
** Ba Shih Intermediate Xingyi Form
** Xingyi Staff Form
** Xingyi Straight Sword Form
** Xingyi 12-Animal Forms
** Xingy Advanced 12-Animal Form "Shi Er Xing"

Baguazhang DVDs
** Bagua Basic Skills
** Basic Building Blocks of Bagua Self-Defense
** 8 Main Palms Form
** Swimming Body Form
** Elk Horn Knives Form

Other DVDs
** Qigong for Stress Management
** Tournament Point Sparring

Ken's DVDs are available on Amazon.com
Also available with Free Shipping Worldwide at www.Kungfu4u.com

ACKNOWLEDGMENTS

A lot of people, including teachers, students and training partners, have contributed to my martial arts journey. I began training in Lexington, Kentucky, my hometown, on September 20, 1973. Over the next 10 years, I trained in Shaolin-Do, Taekwondo and Tien Shan Pai kung-fu. In 1987, I discovered the internal arts with Phillip Starr in Omaha, and began studying Hsing-I, Tai Chi, Bagua, and Qigong. From Starr, I also learned how to make philosophy a key part of my internal arts. In 1991, when I was working as news director of WOI-TV on the Iowa State campus, Coach Terry Dowd saw me practicing in the gym and invited me to train with his Iowa State University boxing team, which I did from age 38 to 40. The young boxers adopted me and I ran stairs, ran the track, did the pushups and crunches, and got in the ring with them. It was fun!

My internal arts journey took a dramatic turn in 1998 when I met Jim and Angela Criscimagna at their home in Rockford, Illinois. I had studied Yang style tai chi for more than a decade and won a gold medal performing the Yang 24 form at the 1990 AAU Kung-Fu National Championships, but within an hour of meeting Jim, and seeing some internal principles demonstrated from Chen tai chi, I knew that I needed to start over.

Through Jim and Angie, I met Ren Guangyi, then Chen Xiaowang. Years later, through another teacher, the late Mark Wasson, I met Chen Xiaoxing and Chen Bing. Two other instructors who have given me valuable insights into body mechanics are Chen Huixian and Michael Chritton, two highly-skilled instructors who live and teach in Overland Park, Kansas.

Mike Sigman deserves credit for his tremendous influence on me in the 1990s. His online listserv, the Neijia List, made me realize the holes that existed in my internal arts knowledge in 1997. When I asked the guys on his listserv to recommend a Chen instructor near me, they suggested Jim and Angie. I also studied Sigman's videos (back in the VHS days) over and over, and attended an outstanding workshop he held in Minneapolis in 2000.

And, of course, my students during the past 21 years deserve my thanks, for pushing me forward and causing me to seek out knowledge and to push my own improvement over the years. Some of my prominent students, also my friends, include Rich Coulter, Chad Steinke, Marilyn Hackett, Colin Frye, Chris Miller, Kim Kruse, and Justin Snow.

But my greatest thanks has to go to my wife, Nancy. The week we met, in August, 2002, she became my biggest kung-fu supporter. Nancy has been beside me ever since. I could not do it without her. My hope is that everyone has a Nancy in their lives. But not this one. This one is mine!

And now, onward and upward, and remember: remain centered at all times.

INTRODUCTION

I was a little surprised that Ken asked me to write an introduction to this book. Most people are looking for well-known masters to increase their legitimacy and promote their works. I am definitely not a master. I am a student.

But perhaps a student is who this book is really meant for. If you were a master, you would already know this stuff.

I have been a student in the martial arts for over 30 years, with experience in a number of different martial arts. I am a perpetual learner because there is so much good stuff out there. During that time I have had a handful of experiences that have changed the way I did just about everything in the martial arts. Watching Ken's Internal Strength DVD and working out with Ken has been one of those experiences.

I had been doing Tai Chi and Baguazhang for close to 20 years before working out with Ken, and the principles he explained to me advanced my understanding of these arts by leaps and bounds after only a few hours.

Ken has a way of explaining fundamental concepts in clear, logical ways that just make sense. They work whether or not you believe in the more mystical trappings that Chinese Internal Arts are often wrapped in, and they get results.

These concepts are not as flashy as the triple spin kicks you can see online, and they are often not readily observable just by watching a YouTube video. These more subtle fundamentals need to be pointed out and explained, and preferably demonstrated in person. A working knowledge of these ideas will pay huge dividends as you advance in your martial arts journey. These concepts will improve the body mechanics and body awareness of just about any martial art that exists.

I have often told less experienced students, "if your basic forms look bad, your advanced forms will look awful." So it is with learning fundamentals. Thanks to Ken's advice, the fundamentals I learned helped to ground my internal forms with improved structure and movement, and set me up for more advanced and subtle forms of power generation.

So from one student to another, I suggest you read this book, study it, and learn from it. It will be well worth your time. I could have saved myself months to years of training if I had known about these fundamentals from the start.

Evan K. Yeung
Tai Chi Chuan student since 1985
Shima-Ha Shorin-Ryu Karate 2nd Dan
Shaolin-Do 1st Dan
Guided Chaos Combatives Instructor
Guided Chaos 2nd Degree Black

1 THE SIX KEY BODY MECHANICS

"What is the Teacher Test?" I asked Jim Criscimagna the day I met him in early 1998. Some Chen Tai Chi guys had been talking about the "Teacher Test" in an online forum called the Neijia List, and they had used strange terms such as "ground path" and "peng jin."

According to what I had read on the Neijia List, any good teacher should be able to pass the Teacher Test, and any new student should ask a teacher to demonstrate it.

"Okay," Jim said. "I'm going to stand with my feet at shoulder width. You can stand at my side."

I had been at Jim's house in Rockford, Illinois for about an hour, after he was recommended to me by the guys on the Neijia List as someone who could explain internal strength, and some of the terms they were using about the internal arts that were foreign to me, even though I had studied the internal arts for more than a decade at that point.

I stood at Jim's side.

"Get into a stance and put your hand on my shoulder," he said.

I got into a typical fighting stance and stretched my arm out, putting my hand on his shoulder.

"Now," he instructed, "without changing your stance or using your arm or shoulder muscles, without cocking your arm back, knock me off my ground."

I tried to comprehend what he was saying. Without changing my stance, and without using my arm and shoulder muscles, and without cocking my arm back, I was to knock him from where he was standing.

About thirty seconds ticked by as I tried to figure out how to knock him off his ground without using my arm and shoulder muscle. What the hell?

Eventually, I laughed.

"I'm paralyzed," I said. "I have no idea what to do."

Jim laughed, too. He directed me to stand with my feet at shoulder width. He stood at my side in a stance and placed his hand on the side of my shoulder.

He appeared to be bowing out his lower back, then he unbowed it and POW! He knocked me off my spot. He had not used the strength of his arm and shoulder muscle to do it. He had not bent his arm and pushed me with it, as I would have done.

"Whole-body movement," he said. "It isn't done with the arm and shoulder."

At that moment, I knew that, after a decade of practice, I had to start over in Tai Chi (Jim spelled it Taiji, and I spell it that way more often now, too, but for this book, I use the commonly known spelling of Tai Chi). I had to learn this "internal strength," and I had to learn Chen style.

Up to this point, my Tai Chi training had been driven by "cultivating chi." As a result, my Tai Chi was weak and empty and my other arts were too "external." I could not find my kua with both hands. They say that when the student is ready, the teacher appears.

I began studying with Jim and Angela Criscimagna.

The Weak Image of the "Soft" Arts

Since beginning my study of the internal arts in 1987, I have read a lot of books and magazine articles about Tai Chi, Xingyi and Bagua. Many of them drown in their desire to be mystical. Others buy into the abstract nature of the old "classics," and instruction is written in a way that no one can understand. In other books, claims are made about benefits that are either false, misleading, or based on anecdotal evidence. Some say you can even use your mind to massage your internal organs and similar nonsense.

One book in my library implies that Tai Chi cured a student's bone cancer. It did not. The author of the Tai Chi book making that claim is dead now. Ironic, isn't it? I think so.

You have not read a book like this one. It might burst some of your belief balloons. I believe the internal arts, especially Tai Chi, attracts too many people who seek the mystical. Ethically-challenged teachers will gladly take money from these gullible people by pretending to have mystical abilities – amazing "chi" power – and some of these teachers make a good living from it.

Many Tai Chi and qigong instructors will tell you that these arts will increase your life expectancy, but if you notice, most Tai Chi instructors and qigong masters die at the same age as other people. My wife's parents died in their 90s and had very few health issues in their later years, and they probably had never even heard of Tai Chi or qigong. Living a long, healthy life is not dependent upon "cultivating chi" with these arts.

The internal arts are not mystical. They are martial arts, designed to break an opponent quickly and put him on the ground. You do not learn a martial art by "cultivating chi." You can do a slow-motion form for a lifetime and never learn how to defend yourself.

People who persist in spreading falsehoods about their abilities and the mysticism of the internal arts have ruined the image of these amazing martial arts. Those people deserve no respect from us.

I studied Yang style Tai Chi for more than a decade before discovering Chen style. I won a gold medal at the 1990 AAU Kung-Fu National Championships in Omaha. I had studied acupuncture for two years, practiced qigong religiously, and practiced my internal arts for at least an hour a day, and sometimes six hours a day. I thought I really knew Tai Chi, Xingyi and Bagua. I was wrong.

The author with Ren Guangyi, Jim Criscimagna and Angela Criscimagna in 2001

After meeting Jim and Angela early in 1998, I studied with them for a few years, then began studying with Mark Wasson, who traveled regularly to the Chen Village to study with the Chen family. Through Jim, Angie and Mark, I was able to learn directly from Chen Xiaowang, Chen Xiaoxing, Chen Bing, Chen Ziqiang, and Ren Guangyi. Later, I learned from Chen Huixian and her husband, Michael Chritton. In 2006, I sponsored Chen Xiaoxing's visa for his visit to hold workshops in the United States. As a thank you, he stayed in our home for a week in Moline, Illinois, practiced with me each day, and held a workshop on Laojia Yilu at our school.

As I studied and learned, I wanted to break down concepts so my students could understand them, in the same way that I would break down a news story for listeners and viewers in my journalism days.

The author being corrected by Chen Xiaoxing in Livermore, CA in 2005

From Mike Sigman, I was introduced to the ground path and peng, and I learned more from Jim and Angie about both of those concepts, plus whole-body movement, san ssu chin (silk-reeling), using the kua and Dantien rotation (there are several ways of spelling Dantien so I picked this one for this book).

Workshops and private lessons from Chen Xiaowang, Chen Xiaoxing, Chen Bing, Chen Ziqiang, Ren Guangyi and Chen Huixian have helped me refine my thinking on these concepts over the years.

Around 2003 to 2006, I developed a curriculum based on this

instruction that emphasizes the teaching of six key body mechanics. By understanding these concepts and methods of movement and body action, you improve your structure and develop the ability to transmit force over a short distance.

We have all heard the stories of a small Chinese man who causes a much larger opponent to go flying by striking him, yet hardly appears to move much at all. This is not the result of something mystical. The old man is not emitting chi. He simply knows the correct body mechanics to deliver power.

It has been my goal to keep improving in these skills, gain deeper insights into them, and pass along those insights to others through blog posts, videos, eBooks, social media posts, and printed books like this one.

One thing to keep in mind is this: any book or video represents a snapshot in time. It shows a student or a "master" at one moment during his or her journey. I am not a master, and do not have the time in this lifetime to become one. I continue to learn and grow in my skill and my understanding of the internal arts. For that reason, this book is a snapshot, and will undergo revision and expansion in future editions as long as I continue progressing.

This book is an attempt to describe, in plain English, the key concepts that I believe internal artists need to know to get started.

The Six Key Body Mechanics

There are six key body mechanics that you must know to begin your quest for high-quality Tai Chi, Xingyi and Bagua. They are:
- Establish and maintain the ground path at all times
- Establish and maintain peng jin at all times
- Use whole-body movement
- Use the spiraling movement of silk-reeling "energy"
- Use the opening and closing of the kua properly
- Use Dantien rotation in all movement

Without any of these six body mechanics, your internal movement will not achieve high-quality. If you are not maintaining the ground path and peng, your movements are empty.

There is only so much a book can do. As we say in the internal arts, "It Has To Be Shown." It is very difficult to convey all of these concepts through a book or a magazine article. The subtleties of movement, the Dantien rotation and the feeling of internal power must be experienced in person.

The Truth about Internal "Energies"

Here is the truth about the "energies" you hear about in Tai Chi and other internal arts. It is true for Peng Jin (ward off energy), Lu Jin (roll back energy) and all the others.

The term "energy" has been misinterpreted. When force is directed at me, I have to decide very quickly how to deal with it. Do I intercept it? Do I deflect it? Do I evade it? And what do I do to counter?

"Split Energy," taking different body parts in two directions.

When force is directed at me, I must decide which "method" I am going to use to defend against it. One method would be to intercept and deflect it, as in roll back energy. If I then step behind my opponent and block his leg as I push his torso backward to take him down, I will be using "split" energy, or Lieh Jin. By taking the upper part of his body backward and the lower part forward, I am "splitting" his energy, as in the photo above.

This is not energy as the literal-minded might think. The word "jin" can also be translated as "power." But for our purposes, it is a skillful method of dealing with an opponent.

You can "pluck" your opponent (Cai or Tsai energy) by suddenly pulling him sharply off-balance, or deflect his punch and deliver an elbow strike (Zhou energy), or bump him with your shoulder, hip, or thigh (Kao energy). All are methods of dealing with force.

Other forms of energy are also "methods" of self-defense. There is Jin Jin, which means "Forward." You are in contact with an opponent and he retreats. That means his energy is withdrawing, so what do you do? You go forward, driving him backward, going with his energy, helping it go where it already wants to go. Likewise, if he is pushing you, instead of pushing back, do Tui energy (Retreat), and withdraw, leading him into emptiness. All of these energies are demonstrated in my videos on "Close-Up Self Defense."

Press 1 – Doing push hands.

Press 2 – Pressing my opponent, making him unable to defend.

Another energy is Ji Jin (pronounced "jee). It is translated as "press energy." But this kind of press is not just the type that happens when you press your hand on someone. Look at the two images on the previous page. Press also means to get close enough that you physically jam your opponent, crowding his space, "squeezing" him and leaving him unable to defend. At that point, he is vulnerable.

Another misinterpreted energy is "Kong Jin," sometimes referred to as "empty force." Some con artists make you think that they can use their chi to knock you down without touching you, and they call it "Empty Force." Here is one real example of empty force. Someone grabs you and exerts force, you push back with force and then you "empty" and put him off-balance. It is the same feeling as if you take a step and suddenly, there is a hole where you thought there was a floor or a sidewalk. By emptying, you put your opponent off-balance long enough to take advantage. See the two images below.

Empty 1 – My partner pushes hard and I return the push to give him a "foundation."

Empty 2 – I release my energy, like removing the floor beneath him, and he loses balance.

The photo "Empty 2" on the previous page is exaggerated. You do not need to move much at all to use "empty" on an opponent. Sometimes, it takes a relaxing of the kua and a subtle release of tension to put your opponent off-balance.

How to Describe Tai Chi, Bagua and Xingyi

Each of the three major internal arts has a unique style of fighting. Tai Chi and Bagua are the closest of the three, sharing many techniques and tactics, while still maintaining their own unique personality. Xingyi is often seen as a bridge between "harder" external arts and more relaxed internal arts. But even though internal arts are described as "soft," there is nothing soft about these arts. Each of them will break you and put you down in a different way.

Tai Chi is like a beach ball that you jump on in a swimming pool. When you jump on a beach ball in the water, it gives and sinks into the water, but it holds its structural integrity. It will only sink so far until pressure builds to the point that it can't go farther. Then it bounces back and spins, dumping you into the water. This is the perfect description of the ground path, peng jin, whole-body movement and silk-reeling energy, which we will discuss in depth later.

Baguazhang is like a spinning wire ball. If you punch into a spinning wire ball, you will get caught in it and you will be tossed out in random directions.

In Tai Chi and Bagua, the main goals are to unbalance and uproot your opponent and control his center. These are close-up fighting arts, designed for grappling range. The closer my opponent gets, the more I can "listen," or feel, what he is doing. I can't "listen" until he touches or grabs me. At that point, I can feel his force and where it is going. In other words, I can feel his energy. It is not mystical.

Xingyiquan is like a bowling ball driving through pins. It powers through them, leaving them scattered and on the ground. It is a wedge that drives through an opponent, taking his ground.

Xingyi is very aggressive. It does not depend on being close enough to "listen" to your opponent's force. Your goal is not necessarily to control his center, as it is in Tai Chi and Bagua. Your opponent is in front of you and you drive through him, with the goal of standing on his ground when you are finished.

Even though Xingyi is more external looking than the other two arts, it relies on the same internal body mechanics. The mechanics may not be quite as obvious sometimes, due to the explosive nature of the art, but they are there, and your Xingyi improves if you focus on the principles in this book.

In the following chapters, I will discuss the concepts, exercises, drills, and techniques that will give you an understanding of the underlying principles for high-quality internal movement. The rest is up to you. A lot of people take these arts up, but very few stay with them long enough to develop skill. Even in the Chen Village, it is said that out of 100 students, only one will develop skill.

At age 48, the author (standing) knocks down a 25-year old karate black belt in a tournament in 2001.

In the end, it is important to remember a few important points:
1. The internal arts rely on physical skills, not metaphysical.
2. Always be wary of anyone who uses the title of "master."
3. Do not check your brains at the door of a martial arts studio. Critical thinking skills are vital. If someone demonstrates or discusses something that is too amazing to be true, it is probably not true.
4. Never put your teacher up on a pedestal. Teachers are human beings; often very flawed human beings.
5. If you have a teacher who does not teach you how to use the art for realistic self-defense, run out of the school and do not go back.

It should not take you 20 years to learn how to use these arts for self-defense. You should be able to apply the internal arts in self-defense within a few weeks; perhaps at a basic level, but even simple techniques and principles can be effective.

I teach my students self-defense from the beginning, but I also teach them the crucial body mechanics that give my students the ability to deliver relaxed power.

This Book is a Woo-Woo Free Zone

Let me make one thing perfectly clear. It does not matter what you "believe." No human being can heal another person by emitting chi (or "qi") into them. No human being, by using their chi, can knock another person down without touching them. No one can touch another person lightly and send them hopping and falling away, unless the person who is hopping and falling is playing along.

There have always been con artists who make money off of gullible people who desperately need to believe in fantasy. But if you notice, these "chi masters" usually will not test their powers on local wrestlers, MMA fighters, or any other skeptical martial artist.

Avoid internal arts teachers who claim to have mystical abilities.

Martial arts teachers who can accomplish fantastic feats of chi would be billionaires if their claims were true. Governments, military leaders and law enforcement agencies from around the world would pay huge sums of money to learn these skills.

Personally, I find it ironic that no one with these abilities has ever become a championship fighter. If I could knock someone down without touching them, or make them hop away if they touch me, I would be the king of the MMA. The fact that none of them have done this should tell you a lot.

And here is another warning. I offer it because I have been there.

If any internal arts teacher tells you that you could get sick or harm your internal organs by doing qigong wrong, or by doing Xingyi fist postures wrong, or by doing any internal arts technique wrong, because it messes up your chi, my advice is to fire them on the spot and find another teacher. Or, if you have friends who believe in this superstitious garbage, I urge you to start running with a smarter crowd, one with more highly-developed critical thinking skills.

The $5,000 Chi Challenge

I have been outspoken on the chi mythology since 2001, when I began offering a $5,000 cash reward to anyone who can knock me down without touching me (using their chi powers). Many pretend to have these powers, but no one has ever taken me up on the offer. They are eager, however, to take money from students who have a psychological need to believe.

There is another psychological factor at work, too. Some of the students who pay money to these "masters" have a need for other people to look at them and say, "He studies with a teacher who has supernatural powers. Perhaps that means HE has supernatural powers, too."

This has no place in the internal arts, but many of us have tolerated it, or refused to call it out, so our arts now attract the gullible and weak-minded who have ruined the image of these arts.

My $5,000 Chi Challenge still stands.

This book is written without the mystical mumbo jumbo so you can see what actually lies at the heart of these powerful self-defense arts. If you are looking for mystical powers, this book is not for you.

The best Chinese internal arts masters do not talk of mystical feats of power. They do not pretend to have mystical abilities. They will tell you that there is only one path to martial arts mastery: very hard work, very hard practice, good instruction and a lot of time.

It's Meditation, Right?

Tai Chi has become a victim of this belief in modern times, but here is my view: you can also take the movements of karate, badminton, baseball or basketball, slow them down and use them for meditation. You would enjoy the same health benefits.

There is nothing magical about Tai Chi. So if you are older and do slow-motion Tai Chi for health and meditation, knock yourself out. Just understand that you are not practicing the complete art unless you are also studying the self-defense applications.

The true "intent" of Tai Chi, Xingyi and Bagua is self-defense. Every movement is intended for this. You do not "detach your mind" to do these arts, you focus on the intent, which is self-defense.

The key to the self-defense applications lies in the body mechanics, which give the movements and the applications their power.

I attended a tournament once, and the panel of judges for forms competition was a mixed group of karate, taekwondo and Shaolin people, but no internal judges.

It was a hot day in a building with no air conditioning, and I was warming up vigorously. When the black belt forms competition began and I was called to perform, I did the Chen 38 form, a beautiful form with slow spiraling and sudden, violent bursts of fajin.

I did not win first place, and one of the judges, a karate black belt, told me, "I marked you off because you were sweating. There is no sweating in Tai Chi."

I did not get upset, because I knew most of the judges had no real understanding of Tai Chi. If you are hot, and are physically active, you sweat! When I have trained with members of the Chen family and their students and disciples, my classmates and I would collapse from leg fatigue at times. We would sweat buckets.

Pain, blood, sweat and exhaustion are required to become skilled at Tai Chi, Xingyi and Bagua. The body gets stronger through pain. As you learn the body mechanics and you hold stances, or do Silk-Reeling exercises or forms very slowly, it is painful and exhausting. But that is how you learn the mechanics. If it is not difficult, and your legs are not burning, then you are taking it far too easy on yourself.

Now that I have outlined what we will study in this book, and what we will *NOT* study, it is time to take the first step in our journey with the foundation of internal strength – the ground path.

2 THE GROUND PATH

Internal strength begins with the ground. But before we tackle the first of the body mechanics, the ground path, I will ask you to check and see if you have developed a very common bad habit.

The Centered Stance

Through every technique, every form, or in any self-defense situation, the internal martial artist seeks to remain mentally and physically centered. If you are defending yourself, and your attacker is attempting to put you off-balance or do you harm, your goal is to maintain your balance or regain it quickly. Practicing these arts and doing activities such as push hands and sparring with partners will help you instinctively find your physical balance, if done correctly.

This book does not deal very much with the mental aspects of centering, but it is all about maintaining a centered stance.

Zhan Zhuang, also called "Standing Stake," is a common internal exercise to accomplish this goal. It is also a qigong exercise. In Tai Chi, the practice of Zhan Zhuang bestows upon you the muscle memory of maintaining a centered stance. In Xingyquan, the San Ti stance is used, and in Baguazhang, the Dragon Stance, or Dragon Posture, is popular. Each of these practices helps build leg strength, helps develop skills with the ground path and peng jin, helps you learn to sink your energy (sink your weight), among other benefits.

It has been reported that many traditional internal arts teachers had their students come to class and hold these stances for weeks, months, even a year or more before they learned any other techniques. That seems like overkill to most of us, but the truth is, these stances build internal and physical strength.

Image S-1 – I ask my martial artist friend Tom to stand straight. Notice how he is naturally leaning back. He THINKS he is straight.

Try this experiment. Ask a martial artist friend to stand straight, with his or her feet at shoulder-width. If you do not have a friend in martial arts, ask anyone to do this.

I can almost guarantee that your friend, whether he studies martial arts or not, will think he is standing straight when, in fact, he is leaning slightly backward.

In the photo above, Image S-1, taken back in 2007 when my hair was a lot darker, the young man I am coaching, Tom Revie, is a black belt in taekwondo, but he wore a white belt out of respect. I asked him to stand straight and put his arms out as if hugging a tree, as we do in Zhan Zhuang. You can see that he is leaning backward. He thinks he is standing straight.

This is how most of us stand until we are corrected and until we develop the muscle memory to put ourselves into a centered stance.

In Image S-2, on the next page, I show why it is not good for self-defense when you stand this way.

Image S-2 – Just a very light push on Tom's chest forces him off-balance backward, causing him to take a step.

When I press very lightly with one finger into Tom's chest in Image S-2, he goes off-balance and has to take a step backward.

One of the first things we do in the internal arts is find a more centered stance. It takes a lot of practice to remain balanced.

Image S-3 – A more centered stance.

In Image S-3, I have asked Tom to slightly flex his knees, and from the waist to the shoulders, tilt slightly forward. When people do this, as Tom does in this photo, they feel as if they are leaning forward, but as you can see, he is straight. I had to tell him to hold his head up and lower his chin slightly. You will probably have to do that with your friends, and someone will have to do it to you, too.

Here is the position I want him to achieve: there should be a straight line from his ear, through his shoulder, through his Huiyin point, and through his ankle, as you can see in Image S-3.

From there, you can sink your weight, sit more into the kua, relax the lower back, tuck the hips, and hold your arms up higher. Every teacher will adjust you differently. The point is: do not lean back, do not lean forward; remain centered. Remember this as we go forward.

You can be centered and balanced even when the weight is on the rear leg. In this photo from a 2006 tournament, my San Ti stance is centered, energy sunk, and intent forward.

Now, On to the Ground Path

The rest of the exercises in this chapter will teach you how to establish and maintain the ground path. In the next chapter, we will introduce the companion to the ground path, which is peng jin.

Every technique, movement and posture in the internal arts depends upon maintaining the ground path and peng at all times.

Many of these exercises will require you to have a partner to push on you, or someone you can pull. This can be a training partner, spouse, relative, friend, or co-worker. Always remember to practice the exercises on both sides, both right and left.

The photos in this section show me with my student and friend, Colin Frye.

Exercise 1 – Grounding to the Shoulder

Your partner should stand sideways to you with his feet parallel, similar to the position of Zhan Zhuang that we set up on page 16. He should relax his knees and sink slightly. His entire body should be relaxed.

Press straight into your partner's shoulder from the side. It should not be too strong a push. The goal is not to push your partner off-balance. It is not a test of your strength. You are not here to win. The goal is for your partner to learn how to establish the ground path.

Image 1 – Pushing into partner's shoulder.

In the image above, I am pushing into Colin's left shoulder. He should feel the push pressing his left foot into the ground. If you drew a diagonal line from his right foot through his left shoulder, that is the vector the ground path is working. Do not push very hard.

Inage 1-A – I am pushing straight in, but the diagonal line shows the vector that takes the force of the push to the ground.

Almost every time you push on a beginner, you can feel them tense up and push back. Just tell them, "Don't push back. Relax, sink, and take it to the ground."

Your partner should stand firm and relaxed, and feel the push press his rear foot into the ground. He should relax his shoulders, his lower back, and his legs. That does not mean he goes limp. He is relaxed but ready. He must sink his weight, or as they say in Tai Chi, "sink your chi." But sinking the chi, or sinking your energy, is simply saying "sink your weight."

If you suddenly let go of his shoulder, your partner should not "spring" back toward you. If he does, that means he is pushing back.

Ask him if he feels the push pressing his opposite foot into the ground.

Another mistake beginners make is that they "collapse" as you push. If he starts caving in, and moving back or inward, away from you, tell him not to collapse.

When my partner tells me that he feels his opposite foot going into the ground, I usually tell him (or her) to very gently push from the grounded foot back up to the shoulder. He will usually push a little too much, so I usually have to say, "Not too much."

When he has established the connection from the grounded foot to the shoulder, I congratulate him. He has just established the ground path. Don't forget to practice on the other side, too.

Solo Exercise

Image 1-C – Using a doorjamb to practice grounding from foot to shoulder.

You can also practice Exercise 1 without a partner. Use a solid object that allows you to get into a good stance and put your shoulder against the object, usually a post or a doorjamb, as in Image 1-C.

Push from the rear foot to the shoulder to establish the ground path. After you feel the connection, back off the heavy pressure and see how light you can push while still feeling your rear foot being pressed slightly into the ground.

That is the connection you need to maintain at all times.

You should practice this exercise until you can establish it on both sides without pushing back. Someone should be able to walk up and suddenly apply a little pressure to your shoulder, and you should be able to ground it without pushing back or collapsing. With a little practice, you can establish the ground path at will. Remember to practice with both sides; both shoulders.

Your job now is to learn to maintain that ground path through every movement, even when walking. There are other exercises in this book that cover this.

What Part of the Foot To Ground From

You might hear different things from different teachers in different arts when it comes to the topic of where to focus the ground in your feet. You might not even hear anything from your teacher about this, but if that is the case, or if your teacher does not know about the ground path, it might be time to find a new teacher.

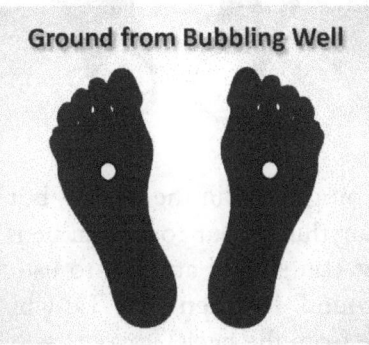

Some teachers say to use the bubbling well point in the feet as the place to put the ground path. The bubbling well point is the first point in the Kidney meridian in acupuncture (Kidney 1), and is located in the depression in the middle of the foot near the ball. This is popular in some styles of Tai Chi. Personally, I do not believe the bubbling well is the best point to focus on in grounding, but that is just my experience.

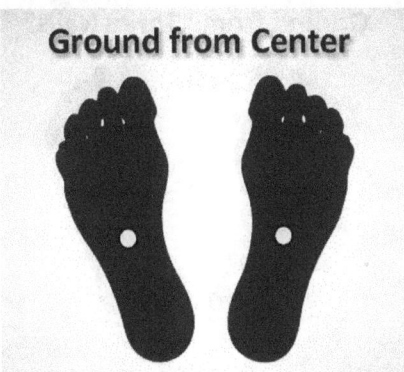

Others say you should ground from the "center" of the feet, in the arch between the heel and the bubbling well point. For a long time, this is where I grounded from, and it is effective.

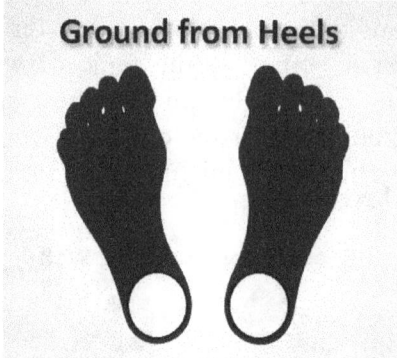

Others say that you ground in the heels – but not the sides or the rear of the heel. If anything, your focus can be is toward the forward part of the heel, but you should attempt to use the entire flat of the heel to meet the ground. In Chen style Tai Chi, some ground from the center and some from the heels.

In recent years, I have switched from grounding from the center of the feet to grounding from the heels. Like any aspect of the internal arts, it takes a while to break old habits. If grounding from the heels, you should make sure that the entire heel is in contact with the ground, and that you do not put your weight in the rear part of the heel at the expense of the front part. You will be unbalanced if you do.

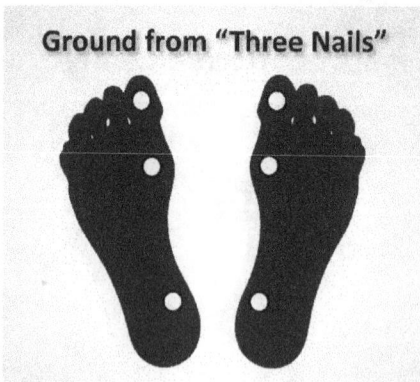

In Yang style Tai Chi, William C.C. Chen uses what he calls the "Three Active Nails." He focuses on the big toe, plus a point on the inner part of the ball of the foot and a point on the inner part of the heel. That view is not shared by all Yang teachers; many believe the foot is rooted through the bubbling well point, but regardless, it is common to hear the phrase, "Strength comes from the ground."

When I studied Yang style, "rooting" was mentioned, but the instructions ran more along mystical lines than practical, something about "imagine your chi is extending 12 feet into the ground like a long pole." It is clear that you can imagine your chi extending hundreds of miles into the ground and that will not give you the ground path, and it will not give you a good root.

In Bagua, the goal is to maintain a "moving root," and that means you should maintain the ground at all times, even when stepping. That is done by making sure the supporting leg is grounded.

If either of these methods works for you, then go for it. I am a big fan of experimenting and trying different methods to see what works for you. But I would urge you to pay special attention to the center of the feet or the heels.

Another important point when standing, stepping or moving in the internal arts is to avoid placing your weight on the edges or the toes of your feet. If you feel one or both of your feet is tilting or rolling toward the inside or outside edge of the foot, you will see the opposite side of the foot, or the opposite side of the shoe, lift slightly off the floor. That is incorrect.

Another mistake I see many beginners make is that they lift their rear heel off the floor when they strike. That is common in some fighting arts, including boxing and Jeet Kune Do, but not in the internal arts. The grounding foot is almost always flat on the ground.

And finally, the toes. Some internal arts classics say to "grip the ground with the toes." This should not be done with muscular force or in an aggressive way. One of the important points to remember is that your toes should not be lifting up off the ground when your foot is planted and grounded.

Chen Changxing wrote, "ten toes should grasp ground." In Xingyi, the toes "grabbing the ground" is a principle of the San Ti stance as taught by the famous master Wang Ji Wu. As usual, do not translate too literally. Each toe touches the ground, but without tension. Because we wear shoes in the Chinese arts, and our toes are not making contact with the ground, it takes focus and practice to get that burned into our muscle memory.

Exercise 2 – Grounding to the Hand

Image 2 – Pushing into his extended hand.

In exercise 2, your partner holds his hand out to the side and you push into his hand (Image 2). His elbow should not be locked out, it should be slightly bent. He can stand with his feet at shoulder width or a wider stance, like a fighting stance.

Press straight into his hand. He should not push back or tense his arm or shoulder muscles. They will remain relaxed and he will focus on "taking it to the ground," trying to feel the same connection as before, this time from his rear foot to his hand. He should relax his lower back and keep his weight sunk.

Remember, if you are pushing into a partner's hand, your push should not be so strong that it will push him back. The goal is to help each other establish the ground path. It will not make anyone Superman, able to resist the strongest push.

Solo Exercise

You can establish and test the ground path when you don't have a partner by using a wall, a post, or, in Image 2-A, a doorjamb. Get into a good stance, hold out your hand and place it on the doorjamb. You can use a palm, a fist, or any hand strike you like.

You push into the object and feel the connection with the rear foot. Maintain a straight, balanced posture and continue pressing, feeling the ground path from the hand to the foot.

Image 2-A – Doing exercise 2 without a partner against a solid object.

Try changing your stance, raising and lowering your body, even stepping sideways, but maintain pressure on the doorjamb and maintain the ground path from the foot to the hand. You are now manipulating the ground (more on that coming up in Exercise 4).

In either the partner exercise or the solo exercise, remember to do both sides.

Exercise 3 – Grounding to the Elbow

Inage 3 – Colin pushes into my elbow with my arm at a 90-degree angle and shoulder-level.

Stand sideways to your partner with one arm out to the side (as in Image 3). You can adopt a high horse stance, a halfway stance, a back stance; anything you want. It is good to experiment with different stances so you can find the ground path in any situation. Your elbow will be level with your shoulder and your arm at a 90-degree angle. Extend the shoulder slightly toward your partner.

In this stance, your partner can push as hard as he wants, and you should be able to take it without collapsing. Practice until you get the right structure.

I have done demonstrations with one person pushing into my elbow, a second person pushing on his back, another person pushing on that person's back, and I have lined up several people and challenged them to push me over. It is a fun demonstration.

In Image 3, Colin pushes into my right elbow and I am taking it to the left foot. It is important in these few exercises that the push comes straight in, so Colin's force should not be going downward or upward, but straight into the elbow.

My position in Image 3 is a powerful stance. Whoever is pushing should feel as if they are pushing into a steel rod. Remember to avoid pushing back. You can close into the left or the right kua (you will understand that more in a later chapter). Relax and let the ground take the push. Keep practicing until you can relax and let the body structure do the work.

Solo Exercise

Image 3-A – Using a doorjamb to test the ground from my rear foot to my elbow.

Just as with Exercise 2, you can do Exercise 3 without a partner by using a wall, a post, or a doorjamb, as in Image 3-A.

Hold your arm at a 90-degree angle to your body and press into the elbow, establishing and maintaining the ground path from the foot to the elbow.

After you establish the ground, and get a good feel for it, experiment with stepping just enough to reposition your body while maintaining contact between your elbow and the object. Do you have to switch the ground path from the rear foot to the front foot at any point when you move? Maintaining the ground is essential in the internal arts, and there is another exercise coming up that explains.

In the end, the purpose of Tai Chi and Bagua for self-defense is not to use force against force. You will not want to push against another push. Instead, you will find ways of neutralizing the push and taking your opponent off-balance so you can counter.

But the ground path, combined with peng jin, gives you internal strength. You may hide this strength at times, such as when you are "yielding" to an opponent's force, but you still maintain the ground at all times, using its strength when you need it.

At this point in your journey, however, the purpose of the ground path exercises is to get your body to feel what you will be aiming to achieve in your internal movement. It may appear relaxed to the observer, especially Tai Chi and Bagua (Xingyi does not always appear relaxed), but behind those graceful movements lies a very strong internal foundation.

Exercise 4 – Ground and Turn

This exercise helps you start learning to maintain the ground path as you move the body into different positions. As you perform the internal arts, it is important to remain relaxed at all times, but maintain a strong body structure – the "iron wrapped in cotton."

Start by having your partner push straight into your elbow, as in Image 4. Your torso should face directly forward.

After you establish the ground path, maintain the ground path and turn your torso to face your partner.

You "break" if at any time during the movement your partner notices that the ground gives way, or your arm pulls inward, resulting in a break in the ground path. You should feel it, too, if what is solid is suddenly not solid. You want to avoid "breaks" in your structure at all times.

Image 4 – In part 1 of this exercise, my torso is facing forward as Colin pushes into my elbow.

Image 4-A – As I maintain the ground through my rear (left) foot, I turn my torso to face my partner.

You can pivot your feet as you turn, but pivot from the heels so you can maintain the ground path.

Exercise 5 – Down and Up Movement

In this exercise, you will move down into your kua and then back up to your original position, maintaining the ground path the entire way.

The kua (pronounced a couple of ways – "kwah" or "gwah") can be thought of as the crease where the thigh meets the groin. It can also be described as the hip socket area. More about the kua in Chapter Four.

Image 5 – My partner pushes directly into my elbow. The knife-edge of my left hand shows where my left kua is located.

Start exercise 5 by having your partner push into your elbow again, as in exercises 3 and 4. Establish the ground path to the rear leg.

Next, close into your left kua (Image 5-A below). You close by relaxing the left hip socket area, including the crease where the thigh meets the groin, and sinking down and into the kua.

Image 5-A – Sinking down and into the left kua, lowering my body while maintaining the ground between my left foot and right shoulder.

Your belly and waist (Dantien area) should turn slightly toward the left kua, but the hips do not turn.

Maintain the ground connection between your left foot and right elbow as you sink into the kua. If you lose your connection, you will feel your elbow lose the connection. Your movement should be slow and smooth while you get the hang of it.

Image 5-B – Return to your original position while maintaining the ground path between the left foot and right shoulder the entire way.

Next, return to your original position, standing up slowly and smoothly while maintaining the ground connection between the foot and the elbow. As you stand, you will open the left kua and relax the right kua. You will feel jerky if you lose the ground path at any time. That's okay, just keep working at it until you can close into the kua as you sink, then return to your original position, all the while maintaining the ground path.

Moving with the ground path is crucial to the internal arts. Practice this exercise on both sides of the body. Let your partner press into your left elbow as you sink into your right kua and return.

If you are pushing on your partner and you feel a break in his ground, call him on it and make him try again.

Notice in all three of the photos, my weight is "sunk." My knees are flexed, not locked out. You rarely lock your legs out in the internal arts, and you rarely stand straight up. Always keep your weight down and knees flexed.

Exercise 6 – Manipulating Ground with Push and Pull

In this exercise, you learn to switch the ground path quickly from the rear leg to the front leg. When you are moving in the internal arts, or when you are in a self-defense situation, the ground path is constantly changing as you adapt to a changing situation.

Image 6-A — Colin pushes straight into my right elbow while I establish the ground path from the left foot.

My partner pushes straight into my right elbow (Image 6-A) as I hold my arm at a 90-degree angle with my elbow at shoulder level. I establish the ground path from the left foot to the right elbow.

Image 6-B — Colin reaches under to pull on my arm, forcing me to change the ground path to the right leg.

Next, my partner reaches under to pull on my arm. I have to switch the ground from my left foot, the rear foot, to my right foot, the front foot. Only by switching the ground can I prevent my partner from pulling me toward him.

Make sure you are not pulling against his pull. Let the ground path do the work as you sink your weight and relax.

This does not make you Superman, so eventually, if he pulls hard enough, he can take you off your ground. That is not the point. His pull should challenge you, but just enough to test your ground path.

How does this work? It is an important concept.

A push from the front is grounded the same as a pull from the rear. A push from the rear is grounded the same as a pull from the front. When someone pushes on your forward elbow, you must ground it through the rear leg. If someone pulls on your forward arm, you must ground it through the front leg.

If someone pushes you from behind, your front leg becomes your rear leg, so you ground a push from behind through the front leg. Likewise, if someone pulls you from behind, you ground it through the rear leg.

Image 6-C – My partner pushes from behind, forcing me to ground it through my left (forward) leg.

In Image 6-C, my partner is pushing from behind. The ground path is between my upper back and my left foot. In these exercises, sink your weight and do not push back.

In the next photo, Image 6-D, Colin grabs my shoulder and pulls, so I ground it to the right leg. In any internal movement, whether it is Tai Chi, Xingyi or Bagua, you are constantly manipulating the ground path.

Image 6-D – My partner pulls from behind, forcing me to ground the pull through the right (rear) leg.

One way to work on this is for your partner to push or pull, then quickly change. If he pushes you from the front or rear, he should suddenly pull, allowing you to practice changing the direction of the ground path. You should practice changing quickly to meet his push or pull.

The purpose of this fast-changing drill is to give you practice in adapting to changing force. The value of that skills will become obvious as you get into other exercises, including push hands or grappling.

This is just a taste of the ground path and a centered stance. We will now add to the body mechanics with an important companion to the ground path: Peng Jin.

3 MAINTAINING PENG JIN

Here is an absolute law of the internal martial arts:

There are many jins (energies or methods), but the most important is Peng Jin.

Before we resume with our internal exercises, I need to stop and explain the second of the six key body mechanics, a skill that always accompanies the ground path.

Every posture and every movement in the internal arts must have both the ground path and Peng Jin. Every one of the internal "energies," or methods of dealing with an opponent's force, involves Peng Jin. You cannot do Lu Jin, Ji Jin, An Jin, Cai Jin, Lieh Jin or any of the others without peng (pronounced "pung").

If your movements do not have both the ground path and peng, your movements and techniques are empty. If you rely on muscular strength to overpower an opponent, you are doing external arts, not internal.

Peng is not that complicated, it is simply foreign to the way most of us in the West are taught to think as we are growing up. We are taught to react to stress and to force with mental and muscular tension. The internal arts, including Qigong, give us a different way of responding to stress and force.

There are teachers who try to make peng seem complicated, abstract, or mystical. The teachers who try to make it complicated attempt to sound like scientists. You don't quite understand what they are saying, but it sounds good. The teachers who make it sound abstract confuse you so that you do not quite understand what they mean, and then there are those who use mystical terms, talking about chi flow and feelings of heat and tingling. You certainly do not have to feel heat or tingling to have good internal structure or movement.

How to Describe Peng Jin

Chen Xiaowang has described it this way:

"Peng Jin is chi flowing, everything full, nothing broken."

In the Chen Xiaowang quote, do not take "chi" literally. I will try to explain it by the end of this chapter. His quote is very important.

Peng Jin is an expansive force, a physical skill that you develop, giving a fullness and a buoyancy to your structure and a feeling that you will not collapse under pressure, even if you "give" a little bit. Some describe it by saying that peng feels as if your body is pumped with air, but that does not quite provide an accurate description.

In the "Eight Energies (Methods)" of Tai Chi, Peng Jin means "ward off." It is an outward, expansive force. That is accurate, but it requires a lot more nuance. Here is the analogy that most accurately describes Peng Jin, and I will illustrate it with images.

Image P-1 — Put a big beach ball or fitness ball into a swimming pool.

Press a beach ball into a swimming pool, as in Image P-1.

Image P-2 – Push the ball into the water as far as you can.

Next, press the beach ball into the water as far as you can. (Image P-2). This will require a lot of energy on your part. You will feel the pressure build, but here is an important point: the ball will give, and it will sink into the water, taking your force, but it will not lose its structural integrity as the potential energy builds with an expansive force. You will reach a point when you cannot push any further.

Image P-3 – Letting go of the ball. The ball springs out of the water.

When you release the ball (Image P-3), the potential energy is released and the ball springs out of the water. This is Peng Jin. It is sometimes described as "concealed strength," and even when doing push hands, or grappling with an opponent, you may choose to hide your peng from your opponent, but it is there, even when you are yielding, ready to release the potential energy when the time is right.

When someone attacks you, what they find should be similar to what you find when you jump onto a beach ball in the water. I'll take a dip and illustrate this concept at the same time.

Image P-4 – I jump onto the ball when it is in the water.

I jump from the side of the pool onto the ball, as in Image P-4. I am much larger and heavier than the ball.

Image P-5 – The ball receives my energy and "gives" with the force.

The ball receives my energy by sinking into the water, but it maintains its structural integrity as it does so. It is still a ball. It is not collapsing, and its potential energy is building.

Image P-6 — The ball releases its potential energy and uses spiraling motion to spin me into the water.

Image P-7 — The ball goes along its merry way, leaving the attacker dumped.

Here is where the analogy adds a little Silk-Reeling Energy, or San Ssu Jin.

As the potential energy in the ball releases, it spirals in a connected way, using the structure of the ball, the force of the energy releasing, and the spiraling movement, making it impossible for me to hang on. The ball has received my energy as far as it can take it, and it puts me off-balance, takes control of my center and spirals me into the water (Images P-6 and P-7).

I invite you to try this experiment yourself. You cannot hang onto the beach ball when it unleashes its built-up energy and spins you.

The internal arts without the ground path and Peng Jin are empty. Without Peng Jin, there is no Tai Chi, no Baguazhang, no Xingyiquan. Peng should flow and be connected throughout every movement, and since there really are no "transitions" in these arts, since every movement in the forms contain fighting applications,

your peng is there at all times. There should be no breaks.
Here is a demonstration of the "Beach Ball" principle at work.

Image P-8 – My partner pushes, but I have peng from my rear leg to my rounded arms.

Image P-9 – Like the beach ball, I "give" and maintain my structural integrity, but I begin spiraling.

In Image P-8, my partner pushes me, but I have Peng Jin and the ground path. In Image P-9, I give a little bit to draw him in, but I begin spiraling and I maintain my structural integrity, my "bubble" of peng.

In this encounter, I am not interested in competing against his muscular force. I want to use his energy against him.

Image P-10 – Like the beach ball, I spin him off-balance, maintaining peng.

Image P-11 – I have spiraled him away and off-balance.

Next, I reach the point when I do not want to go further, and I rotate, spinning his force away (Image P-10), causing him to go off-balance (Image P-11) and giving me a window of opportunity to counter.

It is very important to remember that you must maintain the ground path and Peng Jin throughout every movement.

Xingyiquan is a very explosive martial art. It does not always work the same way as Tai Chi and Baguazhang. The movement in the latter two arts are more subtle than Xingyi.

While a Xingyi fighter drives through his opponent, taking his ground, Tai Chi and Bagua are more likely to intercept or receive an opponent's force and use internal methods to unbalance, uproot, and control the opponent's center, setting up a window to counter-attack, if the opponent is not already on the ground.

So you will not typically go muscle-against-muscle. When someone grabs you in a close-up, grappling-style attack, you rarely use force against force, at least not for long. Sometimes, you give an opponent muscular force to mislead them, giving them a foundation, then you "empty" (Kong Jin) and cause them to go off-balance.

How to Test Peng Jin

One of the important lessons I received from my first Chen Tai Chi instructor, Jim Criscimagna, was one Saturday when he was holding his class in a park. We were practicing Laojia Yilu, and I had just completed the third movement in the form, a movement called "Lazy About Tying the Coat." I was going into the next movement, "Six Sealings and Four Closings."

Jim, who was a good 50 feet away, shouted, "Ken, you lost it!"

I stopped. "Lost what?"

"You lost your peng," he said.

How in the world could he tell from 50 feet away that I had lost my peng, I wondered.

Now, when I watch someone doing any martial art, especially the internal arts, I can easily spot whether they have peng or not.

If someone can walk up and push on your arm, causing your arm to collapse in toward your body, you do not have peng. If you have peng at the end of a movement, but lose it and go a bit limp as you start the next movement, as I did when Jim called me on it in the park, you have lost your peng.

Some internal artists take the word "relaxed" too literally. Relaxed power does not mean limp power.

When you have peng, it is as if you have been pumped with air. If your arms are rounded, for example, and someone pushes on your forearm, it is as if they are pressing into the beach ball. There might be a slight buoyancy to it, but you can feel the ground and it feels solid, maintaining its structural integrity.

When you do not have peng, and someone pushes on your

forearm, your arm may collapse toward your chest, allowing them to pin your arm against your chest. In the next few photos, I will attempt to demonstrate the difference between "chi flow" and having no chi flow.

Image P-12 – My partner pushes and I collapse because I have no peng.

Image P-13 – With no peng connected to the ground, I am pushed off-balance.

In Image P-12 and P-13, my partner pushes and there is no peng, so I collapse, making it easy for him to do with me what he wants.

Peng does not mean tense. It is not muscular tension. It is an expansive feeling, connected to the ground. The ground path is crucial for establishing and maintaining Peng Jin through your body.

Image P-14 – My partner pushes, but I connect the ground from my rear foot (left foot in this photo) to my right elbow/forearm.

In Image P-14, my partner pushes, but I maintain peng, along with the ground path. You can almost think of it as a "bubble" around me that he cannot break through, but it is a bubble that I create through physical practice of relaxed strength that connects to the ground.

This is the difference between "chi flow" (Image P-14) which includes good structure, and no chi flow (Images P-12 and P-13) where the peng, and thus the structure, is weak.

If I can connect my arms to the ground, I can remain relaxed and still have the "iron wrapped in cotton" that provides solid structure to all of my internal movements. There is nothing "soft" about it.

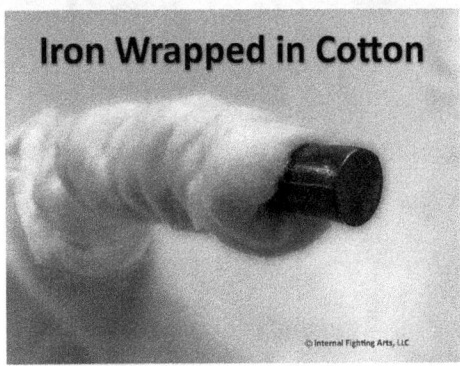

Remember Chen Xiaowang's definition of Peng Jin that I put on page 35? "Peng Jin is chi flowing, everything full, nothing broken."

You can see everything is not full in Images P-12 and P-13. But chi is flowing in Image P-14 because there is solid structure and Peng Jin.

Image P-15 – Limp arm with no peng connected to the ground.

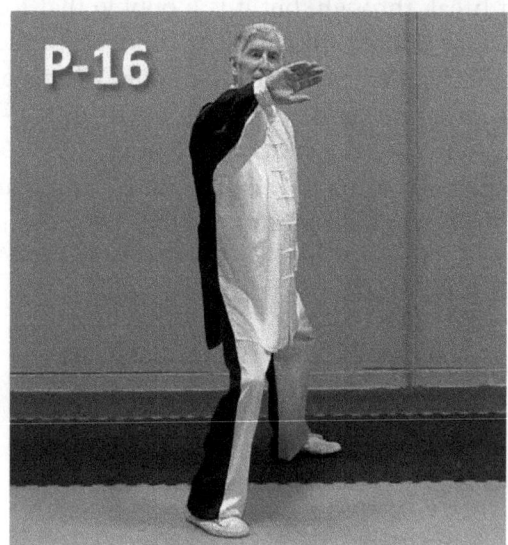

Image P-16 – Everything full, nothing broken. Peng is connected to the ground.

Occasionally, I see Tai Chi being performed without peng, but if you talk to the person doing the form, he will swear he has peng. "We hide it," he might say. No, actually, if someone with an experienced eye is unable to see it, you probably do not have it.

Maintain Peng Throughout the Body

Your Tai Chi is stronger if you maintain peng in the legs. When you see someone performing Tai Chi and their knees collapse, they are losing peng. I will demonstrate in the next few images.

Image P-17 – Notice the fullness, the peng in both legs.

Image P-18 – Shifting the weight from right to left, but maintaining peng in both legs.

In this part of a silk-reeling exercise, which is called "Double Hand Reeling," Image P-17 and P-18 show a movement that shifts weight from the right leg to the left leg. Notice how strong the posture is in the legs. Now, I will demonstrate weakness in your structure.

Image P-19 – This is wrong; collapsing the right leg as I shift to the left.

Do you see the difference between the right leg in P-18 and the right leg in P-19? In the latter image, the leg is more vulnerable. Once the leg collapses, the peng collapses, and you cannot defend as well or as completely as you can in the position in P-17 and P-18.

You will see Tai Chi students and even masters committing this mistake. Here is another place it is done in Chen style, during the movement, "Buddha's Warrior Attendant Pounds Mortar."

Image P-20 – A collapsed left knee in "Buddha's Warrior." Not good.

Image P-21 — Instead of collapsing, I maintain peng in the leg.

Image P-21 is a better representation of maintaining peng in the legs. It should be easy to see the difference in the left leg in this image and in P-20.

As I write this book, I was alerted to a YouTube video of the student of a tai chi master who is doing a form, and his right knee is collapsed so badly during Single Whip, it looks as if it is almost touching the ground. Somewhere along the line, an important quality got lost in translation. And if your Chinese master is collapsing his legs during a posture, who is going to correct him?

The Trunk of the Tree is Solid

I have heard Chen Xiaowang say that our legs are like the trunk of a tree – solid and rooted. The upper part of the body, including the torso and arms, are the branches of the tree. They move and bend to outside forces such as wind while the tree remains solidly rooted in the ground. Now, imagine how rooted the trunk of the tree can be if the bottom part of the trunk is losing its root by bending to the ground while the branches are waving in the wind above.

None of this is mysterious, but it is difficult to rewire our brains and learn new, relaxed ways of moving that are different than the way we were taught growing up. It requires a lot of practice, focusing on maintaining peng and utilizing the ground path at all times.

Exercise 7 – Putting Peng in Other Parts of Body

There is a saying in the internal arts that you use "whole body as fist." This means that you can channel internal strength to any part of the body for the "iron wrapped in cotton," and the ability to deliver power.

Returning to our exercises, we already showed how to use the ground path to the shoulder, elbow and arm (see Chapter 2 for exercises one through three). You can actually put ground and peng anywhere.

Image 7 – "Filling up" the ribcage with ground from the left foot and peng jin.

Have your partner press into your ribcage as in Image 7. It should not be a hard push intended to move you off your spot. Instead, it is a steady pressure, intended to test your ability to ground.

At first, you should stand normally. You will feel the ribcage give a little under the pressure.

Next, take the push to the ground. If your partner is pressing into your right ribcage, you should take it to the left foot, as in Image 7.

Fill the ribcage with peng, and connect that peng to the ground. To your partner, it will feel as if your ribcage is filling up. It will become more solid, and he will feel as if he is pressing against a solid object.

Do not stick out the hip or move the leg. Just "fill up" the ribcage with the ground path from the left foot and with peng.

The ability to "fill up" parts of your body with peng, and connect it to the ground, is an important internal skill. It is a physical skill. You are not filling up with anything mystical, and once you feel it, you will understand.

You can bump an opponent with your ribcage. You can also bump with your hip. I had a student in a vulnerable position just a few days ago, as I write this. I bumped the back of his leg with my thigh and broke his structure enough to take him down.

The two most important skills in the internal arts are to combine the ground path with Peng Jin at all times, in all movements.

Combining Peng Jin with the Ground Path

Chen Xiaowang also tells a great story to describe the ground path as it relates to Peng Jin.

Imagine lifting a car off the ground and revving the engine as hard as it will go. The engine will make a lot of noise, and if you put it into Drive, the wheels will be turning like crazy, but the car will go nowhere. That is peng jin. It is useless until you add one more thing.

Now put the car on the ground and you will see the power come to life as it gets traction. That is the ground path at work, and that is how the ground powers our techniques, by providing the foundation for our internal strength to flow.

In the next chapter, we will explore another important skill you need for high-quality internal gongfu — opening and closing the kua. If the legs are like the trunk of a tree, keeping you solidly rooted to the ground, the kua acts like a buoy in the water, allowing you to adjust to changing forces. I may be mixing metaphors, but it works.

After learning the importance of the kua, followed by Dantien rotation, we will be ready to begin putting the concepts into action in other exercises that will develop your internal movement and power, putting all the body mechanics to work.

4 INTERNAL MOVEMENT AND THE KUA

It has been said that if you understand the kua, you understand Tai Chi. The kua (pronounced "gwah" or "kwah") is in the area of the crease at the top of the legs at the groin, in and around the hip socket. It is sometimes said to be the area of the ball joint, where the leg meets the hip, or the area of the inguinal ligament (see next page).

In the internal arts – Tai Chi, Xingyi and Bagua – you are constantly opening one kua and closing the other. As you shift the weight, you are opening and closing the kua. Learning to do this properly is an art in itself.

Image K-1 – My hands are placed along the crease at the top of the legs. This is the area, running through the hip socket, that is known as the kua.

Here are a couple of photos from Gray's Anatomy, showing the Inguinal Ligament, running diagonally. This is the area of the kua.

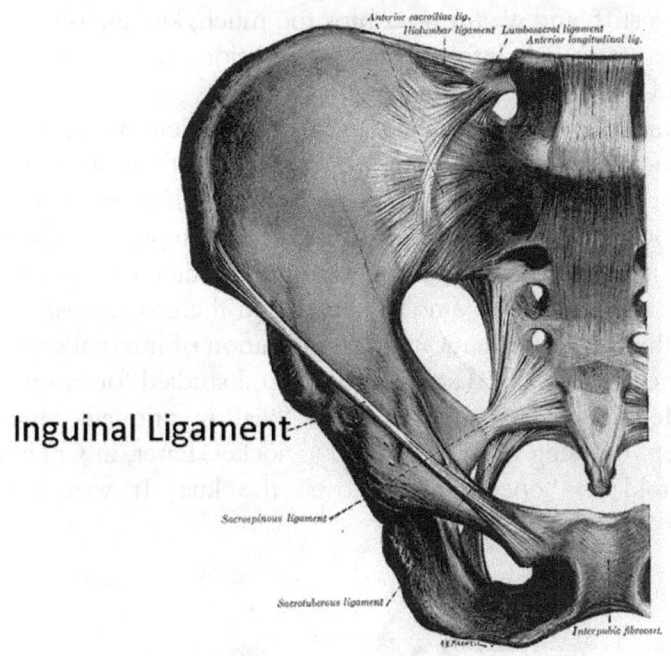

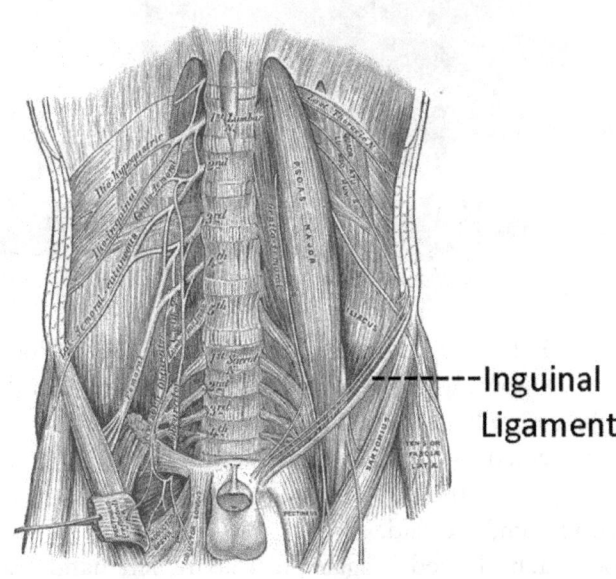

When we begin learning the internal arts, one of the common problems we have, whether we realize it or not, is a stiffness in the joints. Our wrists are too stiff, especially among men; our shoulders are too stiff, and we turn our hips too much, kinking our posture and twisting ourselves into unbalanced positions from which we cannot defend..

Some internal arts teachers make the problem worse, because they tell students to turn their hips when they turn their Dantien.

When learning to use the kua, you must differentiate between the hip socket region, the legs, the waist and hips, and the torso. By learning to use the kua properly, you coordinate the upper and lower body, and are able to smoothly maintain the ground path, peng, and the other body mechanics in the application of internal strength.

When I first started studying Tai Chi, I studied for more than a decade and never heard the word "kua" mentioned. There was no concept of using the area at the hip socket. Later, in Chen Tai Chi, I was told to "open" and "close" the kua. It was not easy to understand.

The author and Grandmaster Chen Xiaowang in 2003.

In 2003, I was performing the Hidden Hand Punch in front of Chen Xiaowang in a workshop on the Laojia Yilu form. Grandmaster Chen was having each of us do the movement for him as he corrected us. I cranked the hands and closed into the right kua, preparing to fire the punch. He stopped me.

"Too much," he said.

Too much? I tried it again, feet apart, left hand cranking with an open palm, right hand making a fist, and I closed into the right kua.

"Too much," he repeated, shaking his head.

Grandmaster Chen demonstrated, getting into position, and as he spiraled the hands, he relaxed softly into the right kua. He looked at me, then demonstrated the way I did it. "Too much," he said. Then he did it again his way, gently. "Just enough," he said softly.

I got the message. "Too much" meant I was closing too hard, in an exaggerated way. His closing was easy to see, but more subtle.

Image K-2 – Closing "too much" into the right kua before "Hidden Hand Punch."

Image K-3 – Closing "just enough" into the right kua.

He was unable to put it into plain English or to explain in depth, so for the next few years, I worked on trying not to do more than "just enough." Each time I did kua movements, I kept thinking, "Too much" and kept working to find "just enough."

"Relax the Hip"

Years later, I was training at a workshop in Madison, Wisconsin with Chen Huixian and her husband, Michael Chritton, world-class teachers who live in the Overland Park, Kansas area (kctaiji.com).

The author being corrected by Chen Huixian in 2013.

At this workshop, Huixian was coaching us in a movement, and at the very beginning of the move she said, "Relax the hip."

I had a flash of satori, enlightenment. The sky opened, and the Universal Life Force came rushing down and opened my eyes so I could finally see. My chi burst like multi-colored confetti into the air.

Okay, that's a big over-the-top. Let's just say that the light bulb flashed on in my brain.

Relax the hip! This was the difference. By "relaxing the hip," you close the kua without being "too much." It is "just enough."

The Kua -- Relaxing and Sitting

"Song Kua" is the ability to remain loose and relaxed in the kua. By remaining relaxed, you have more freedom of motion. Motion is restricted if you are tense or tight through the waist and kua area.

"Zuo Kua" means that you "sit" into the kua. It almost appears as if you are sitting in a chair. Like all the body mechanics in the internal arts, you must be relaxed to have both Song Kua and Zuo Kua.

Image K-4 -- Not sitting into the kua. Notice the "V" at the crotch.

*Image K-5 – Sitting into the kua, like sitting on a chair.
Notice the rounded area at the crotch.*

So you must "relax the hip" in the area of the Inguinal Ligament, the crease where the leg meets the groin and hip. It is subtle, and it takes a lot of practice to learn to isolate that area and relax it rather than doing "too much" and working the musculature. As you close into one kua, the other one opens, and you feel a slight stretch in the ligament area as it opens.

These are important concepts for Xingyi, Tai Chi and Bagua. Below are pictures from a Bagua movement called "Sweep the Rider from the Horse."

Image K-6 – "Sweep the Rider" often comes after "Push the Mountain."

Image K-7 – I relax and close more into the right kua as I turn the waist and knock my imaginary opponent over my leg.

I am sitting into the kua in both photos, but I sit even more in Image K-7. Notice the rounded area at the crotch. That is what you want, not the "V" as in Image K-4 (on the previous page). In Image K-7, the right kua is closed and the left kua is open.

The next image shows a common mistake that beginners make.

Image K-8 – Compare this photo to Image K-7. In this image, the hips are turned too much and the left leg is collapsing.

In Image K-8, I am closing into the right kua to sweep the rider, but I am turning my left leg too far, I have closed "too much" into the right kua, and my hips have turned too much. Notice also that my left leg is on the verge of collapsing, instead of maintaining peng as in Image K-7.

The lower body needs to move a little, and the legs need to spiral, otherwise there would be no "whole-body movement." But when you take it too far, it results in a broken structure and you put yourself in a vulnerable position.

Monkey Doesn't Want to Go to School

Here is a fun exercise that helps you understand the value of Zuo Kua – sitting into the kua. The exercise is called "Monkey Doesn't Want to Go to School." Based on my memories of school when I was a kid, I think I was a monkey, because I certainly did not want to go.

To do this exercise, get into a wide stance, similar to the one at the end of Single Whip, or on the previous page in the "Sweep the Rider" position.

Your partner will pull on your front arm. You will find that if you sink your energy, relax into the kua, and sit into the rear kua (the left kua in the photos below), it becomes much harder for your partner to pull you off your ground. Your partner should pull with a steady force, not a jerk, but he or she should pull with increasing strength as you sit and sink, and ground from the front leg.

Image K-9 – My partner pulls on me as I sit into the left kua.

Image K-10 – He pulls harder. The monkey does not want to go to school. I ground from the right leg, sink my energy and sit back into the rear (left) kua.

The principles in this book will not make you superhuman. It is possible for Colin to pull hard enough to cause me to move forward. Someone larger would still have difficulty, but they could move me if they tried hard enough.

The purpose of these principles is not to resist force. For example, if someone really tried to pull me this hard, I would go with it and cause them to go off-balance backward.

The purpose is to show you the internal strength that you develop through proper structure and the six key body mechanics we are focusing on in this book. As you learn to "listen" to an opponent's force, adapt to it, adhere to it, follow it, neutralize it, and counter it, these internal body mechanics will play an important role.

The Buoy in the Ocean

Think of the kua this way: by using it properly, it is constantly adjusting to changing force, keeping you centered and upright, like a buoy in the ocean.

A buoy in the ocean adapts to constantly changing energy from the water and remains upright.

As your opponent's force changes and adapts to your actions and reactions, you make micro-adjustments in your kua, your stance, and your position. Your purpose is to maintain your physical balance.

One of the goals of an internal arts fighter is to prevent your opponent from finding your center. If you are stiff in the kua, hips and upper body, it is easy for your opponent to connect with your center and push or pull you off-balance.

If you relax the kua and torso when your opponent pushes on you, he will not be able to find your center and push you off-balance.

An Exercise from Chen Bing

I learned this exercise from Chen Bing in 2005 as we were practicing push hands. To be effective in the internal arts, you must prevent your opponent from finding your center. This exercise helps.

The author with Chen Bing in Chicago, 2005.

The goal is to find your opponent's center and push him off his spot, while preventing him from finding your center.

Pushing Chen Bing was like trying to push a rag doll. Each time I pushed, he disappeared beneath my hand. I could not find his center, but anytime he tried, he found my center and pushed me off my spot. He was reacting with relaxation, I was reacting with tension.

Image K-11 – Right feet out, one hand on partner's chest near the shoulder.

Stand with a partner as if doing single-hand push hands, as in Image K-11. Place your right hand on his chest near his left shoulder. He places his right hand on the same place on your chest.

Image K-12 – Try to push each other off-balance by finding your partner's center.

As your partner pushes you, sink your energy, relax the body, turn the waist and relax the kua to keep him from finding your center. If you stiffen, or if you let him turn you too far, you will become "double weighted" and unable to defend. He will find your center and you will be pushed off-balance. Meet force with relaxation and let your kua and body make adjustments to maintain your center.

Image K-12-A – Colin stiffens, allowing me to find his center, pushing him off-balance.

Does This Posture Make My Butt Look Big?

Sticking out the butt is a mistake a lot of us make early in our training, until somebody yells at us. Image K-13 is a common sight among new students. This is the posture for "Lazy About Tying the Coat." In Image K-14, we see that I have straightened my posture, relaxed the lower back, and allowed the buttocks to drop.

It is almost impossible to open and close the kua properly if your lower back and butt are not right. Try it yourself and you will see.

Image K-13 – It is difficult to use the kua properly until your lower back is relaxed and your buttocks are not protruding.

Image K-14 – Relaxing the lower back and tucking the buttocks, the way it should be.

Rounding the Crotch

I was practicing one night and my wife asked what I was doing.

"I'm rounding my crotch," I said. She reached for the phone to call her attorney, but I stopped her to explain.

When you are upright in a Tai Chi posture, your groin should be rounded like an arch instead of an inverted V. Look at the images below.

Notice the inverted V in the first image above, when I am not rounded, compared with the lower image. But even if you are in a higher stance than I am in the "Rounded" photo, you can still round the groin by relaxing and sinking into the kua.

Using the kua properly, using the other body mechanics taught in this book, and maintaining good structure will push your martial arts to a higher level. You will be stronger and yet more flexible.

Strength is not rigid. As the old Taoist saying, repeated by Bruce Lee goes, "The softest thing cannot be snapped."

Adapting and adjusting, yielding, maintaining and recovering your equilibrium like the buoy in the ocean, and always maintaining the iron beneath the cotton, we hold our structural integrity and maintain our mental and physical balance while our opponent loses his.

It is not easy to achieve. It takes years of practice, deep thought and reflection in a quiet place.

Early on in your training, there are so many things to think about when trying to do a form properly, you can become paralyzed if you think about it all while practicing a series of movements.

One of the training methods I have used is to focus on one aspect of posture or mechanics as I do a form. For example, I will do a form and focus throughout each movement on opening and closing the kua properly. If any particular movement does not feel right, I will practice it over again until it does feel right, then I will move on. The next time I do the form, I might focus on maintaining ground and peng throughout. The next time, I might focus on the spiraling. The next time, I will focus on something else, perhaps Dantien rotation.

Gradually, you get each skill down, and your form gets better and better, one baby step at a time.

In the next chapter, we look at the Dantien. I often spell it Dan T'ien, but for this book it is Dantien. The kua and the Dantien are closely connected in internal movement. When the kua closes, it initiates the rotating of the Dantien. Try it yourself. Stand in a position and relax one kua. Notice the Dantien begins rotating toward the closing kua.

Now that you understand the way the kua works, it is time to get into Dantien rotation.

5 DANTIEN ROTATION

The Dantien is the "field of elixir" in Traditional Chinese Medicine (TCM). According to tradition and mythology, energy comes into the body and is stored in the Dantien. From there, they believe, chi circulates through the meridians.

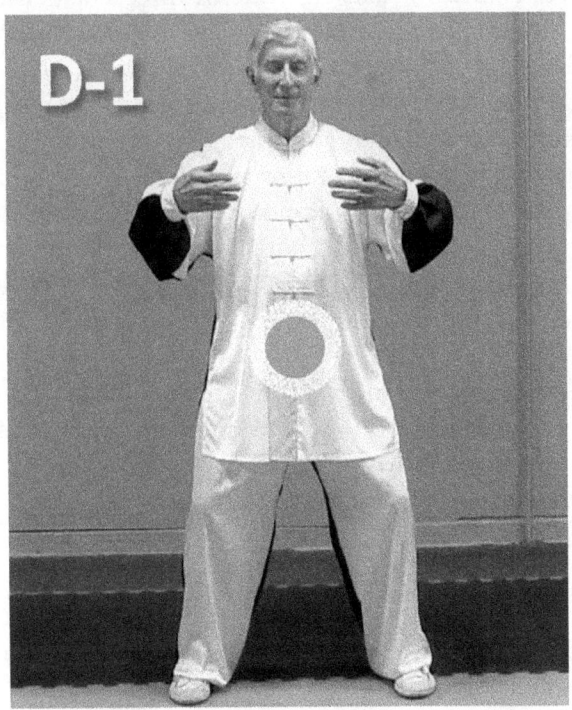

Image D-1 – Location of Lower Dantien, below navel and inside body.

I heard Chen Xiaowang say, "You do not need to believe in chi to do good Tai Chi." He knows that if you get the body mechanics and structure, your Tai Chi will be high-quality.

I do not believe in the literal scientific reality of a Dantien. As a 21st Century, college-educated American who applies critical thinking skills and expects evidence before I cling to a belief, there is no evidence whatsoever that our bodies contain "chi" (also spelled "qi") or a Dantien at any level – low, middle or high.

Some people will tell you that you must control your fascia to control your Dantien. That is "poppycock." You can no more control your fascia than you can control your skin. Your fascia is there. If you stretch out your arm, you can feel the stretch. Your skin stretches, too, but you have no "control" over your skin. The same is true with fascia.

However, chi can serve as a great mental visualization tool, and the Dantien, particularly the musculature in the area of the Lower Dantien, is important in the movement of the internal arts. I will try to explain why in this chapter.

The Lower Dantien is allegedly one of three Dantiens, which also include the Middle Dantien (at chest level) and the Upper Dantien (forehead level). The Lower Dantien is located a couple of finger-widths below the navel and a couple of finger-widths inside the body. It is approximately the size of your fist.

The first thing you need to know is this: there is nothing mystical about using the Dantien. You do not need to "cultivate chi" to use it. Instead, you need to control your core muscles and integrate the movement of your core with the whole body, connected to the ground and working in conjunction with the other internal body mechanics.

If you have ever stood in front of a mirror and sucked in your gut, then let it go so it falls, you are working your Dantien. Like a belly dancer, you will learn to move the muscles below the navel in different directions to match and to lead your body's movement.

One Principle and Three Techniques

Chen Xiaowang says Tai Chi (Taiji) is made up of "One principle and three techniques."

This One Principle and Three Techniques should be part of the focus of your Xingyi, your Tai Chi, and your Bagua movement. When one part moves, all parts move. Your Dantien rotates throughout each movement.

The One Principle: When one part moves, all parts move, and the Dantien leads all movement. This principle is extremely important, and is the concept behind two of the body mechanics discussed in this book: Dantien rotation and whole-body movement.

First Technique: The Dantien rotates in a forward circle on a vertical axis, up the back and down the front, or a backward circle, up the front and down the back.

Second Technique: The Dantien rotates in a circle on a horizontal axis to the left or the right.

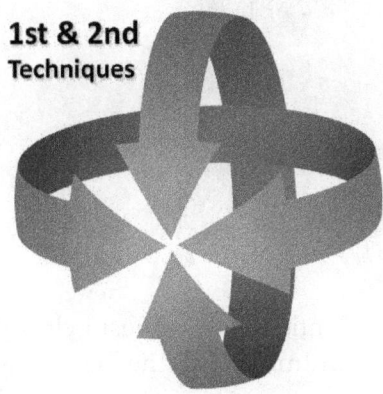

Third Technique: The Dantien rotates in a combination of the other directions, and diagonally.

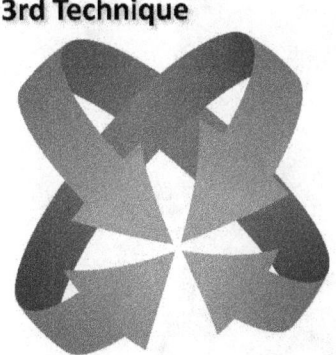

Dantien rotation is one of the skills that requires the most practice in the internal arts. But how do you actually "rotate" the Dantien? I'm glad you asked. You use the musculature below the navel and move it inward (like sucking in your gut), upward, outward (pushing your belly out) and downward (letting your gut relax and drop). I'll show you from a side angle, doing a vertical rotation from front to back, up, and then to front and down again.

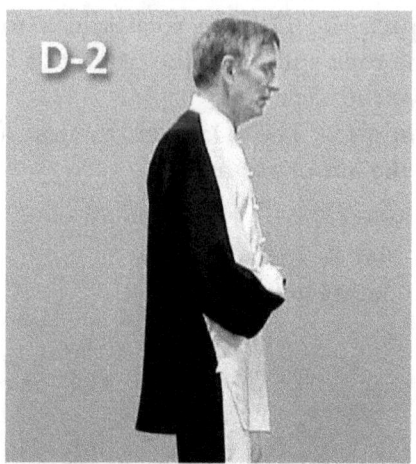

Image D-2 – The Dantien is just below the navel and inside the body.

In Image D-2 the Dantien, the area just below the navel, is relaxed and in a normal state. In Image D-3, the Dantien is pulled inward.

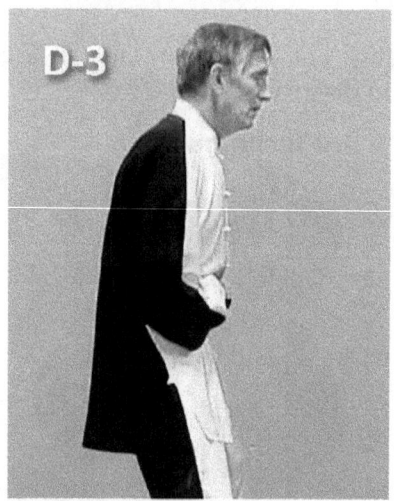

Image D-3 – The Dantien is pulled inward, like sucking in your gut. The lower back bows out.

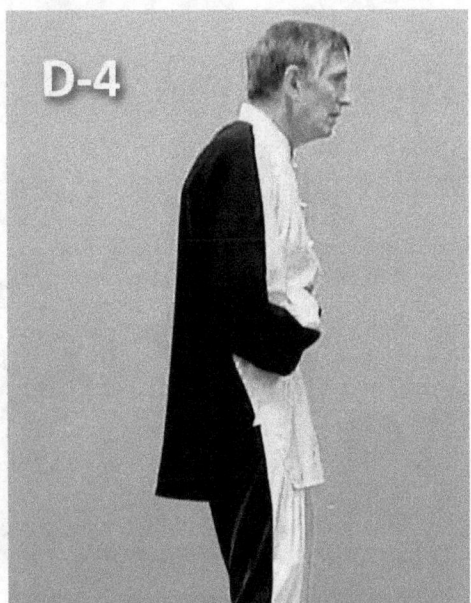

Image D-4 – Raise the musculature in the Dantien area upward.

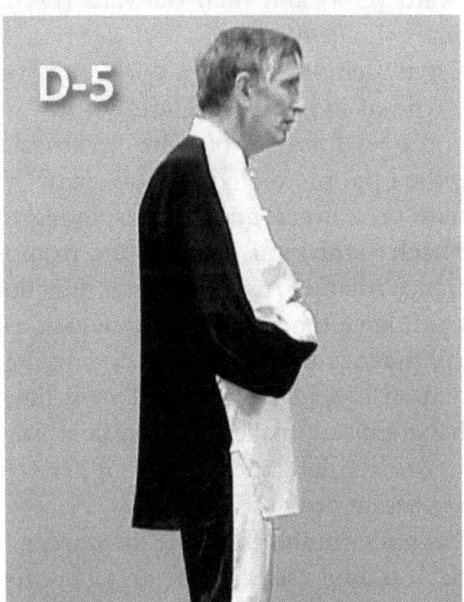

Image D-5 – After pulling the Dantien upward, push it outward. The lower back is unbowing.

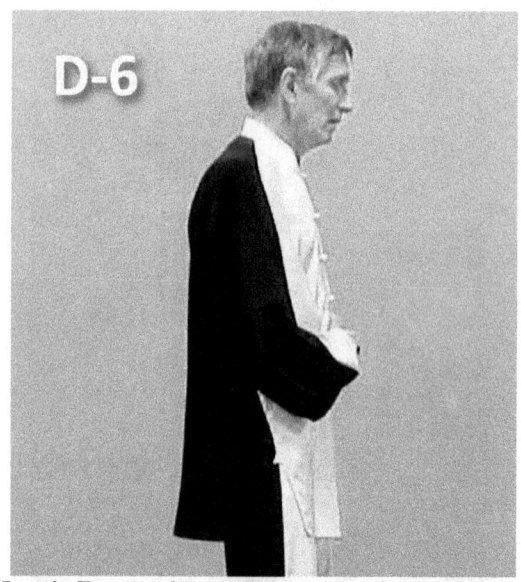

Image D-6 – Let the Dantien drop, and now you are back in your original position.

Continuing the rotation in Images D-4 and D-5, you move the musculature upward (D-4) and then outward (D-5). In Image D-6, you let it drop down the front side.

This is not easy to demonstrate in a book, but you should be able to do that same type of muscular rotation not just in a vertical circle where the rotation goes forward, but also a vertical circle where the rotation is going the opposite direction; backward.

Next, you rotate on a horizontal circle, rotating to the left, to the back, across the back to the right, then around front to the left again.

Then, you practice rotating in the opposite direction.

At that point you have the first two techniques, as shown on page 64. Next, you will practice rotating and changing the direction in the middle of the rotation – including angles. That is the third technique.

Here is another rotation (images start on next page). You go from the bottom center to the left, then to the upper center, then to the right, then to the bottom center.

It is a circle that goes around from the lower part of the center, left to right and back. It is a lot easier to see on video than in still images, but check out the photos starting with Image D-6-A.

Image D-6-A -- Place your hands on the Dantien area. This can also be a Silk-Reeling exercise. The circle shows the direction the Dantien will be rotating.

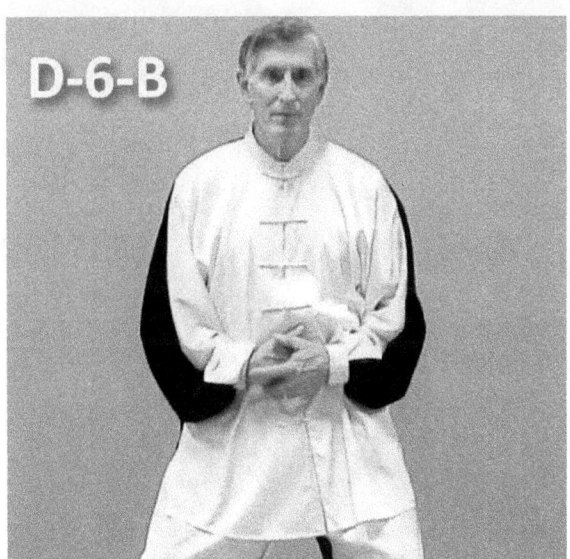

Image D-6-B – Rotate the Dantien to the left. You are not turning the hips or the waist, but you can close into the left kua as the Dantien rotates in that direction.

Start with your weight even (Image D-6-A), then with the ground connected from the right foot, relax the left kua and let the Dantien rotate to the left (Image D-6-B).

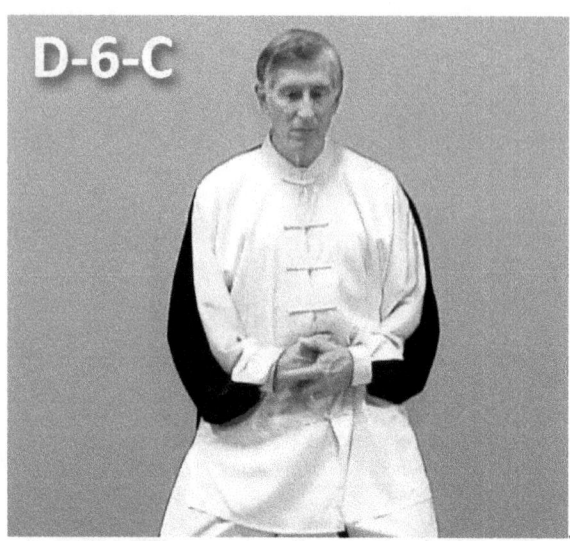

Image D-6-C – Shifting the ground path to the left foot, connect it to the Dantien and lift it up over the top and toward the right kua.

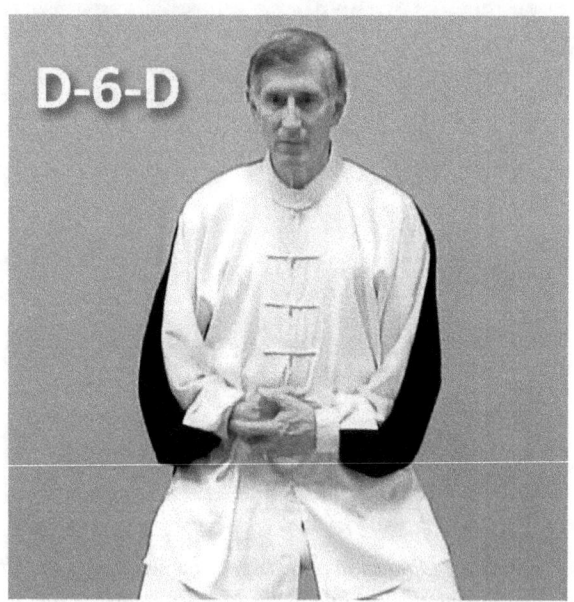

Image D-6-D – Relax the right kua and rotate the Dantien to the right. As it comes down on the right side, you start compressing into the right leg.

After the Dantien goes left, connect the ground from the left foot and lift the Dantien up and over the top of the circle toward the right (Image D-6-C). After the Dantien passes the upper center, relax the right kua (Image D-6-D), which will assist the Dantien in its journey around the circle.

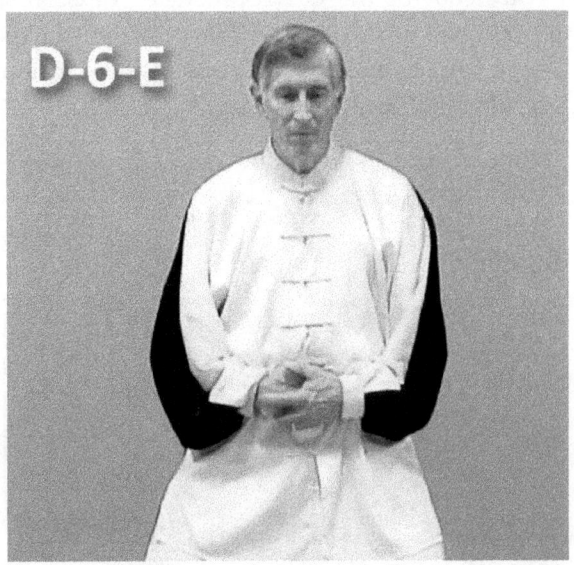

Image D-6-E – Circling along the bottom, the Dantien reaches the center. Continue on with more repetitions, or go the opposite direction.

The Dantien returns to the center (Image D-6-E). You can rotate the Dantien in horizontal circles, vertical circles, just about any combination of directions you can think of. They all may come in handy at the right time.

Bowing and Unbowing the Lower Back

When you put all the internal body mechanics together, you are delivering strength from the ground through the body in a connected ribbon of power through the body in a "wave."

When you do this very fast, in an explosive burst of power, it is called "fajin" ("issuing energy"). At that point, you are incorporating all six internal body mechanics at a very fast speed. It is the same as when you do the movement very slowly, except this time, you "put on the gas," as Chen Xiaowang would say.

Many people do not understand why Tai Chi is often done very slowly. That is to master the body mechanics, so when you "put on the gas," the power will be there at fast speed. If you don't practice long enough to get the body mechanics at slow speeds, your power will fall apart at fast speeds. With that in mind, here is another bit of information you need for the development of internal strength and the mechanics that will give you good power when you speed it up.

Delivering smooth, connected power – fajin -- often involves a bowing and unbowing of the lower back.

As internal strength flows from the ground through the body, the power often stores in the lower back before releasing, much like the string of an archer's bow.

A perfect analogy for this bowing and unbowing is the "store and release" of an archer's bow. The power builds as the string is pulled back. It is potential energy, like the power that builds when you push the beach ball into the water, as we saw in the chapter on Peng Jin.

When you strike, the unbowing of the back, like the release of the string, combined with the ground path and other mechanics, helps fire the force through the part of your body that is striking.

Fajin happens when there is a store and release through the body. It generally happens much faster than pulling a bow, and the body mechanics are often so subtle, they can be difficult to recognize. That is one reason that when a little old Chinese master knocks a big guy a few feet back, people proclaim that the old man has "powerful chi." That definition is fantasy. He probably just has great body mechanics. The use of the Dantien is part of that process.

Bowing and unbowing the lower back is crucial for Xingyi, Tai Chi and Bagua. I will demonstrate on the next page in an exercise you can do almost anytime you open a door that swings away from you.

I will exaggerate the action in the back during the release of energy. I will do an internal strength exercise pretending Colin is a door

(Image D-7 below). I am going to knock him away without changing my stance or using localized arm or shoulder muscle.

Image D-7 – In this exercise, my partner stands like a door. I want to knock him away without changing my stance or using arm/shoulder muscle.

I am sitting deep into the kua and the ground path goes from the left foot through the hands. Notice Colin is standing with feet parallel. I am exaggerating in these photos to get the point across.

Image D-8 – I push off the left leg and let the lower back bow out.

When you sink your energy as it shows in Image D-7 (you actually do not have to go that low), even if it not that pronounced, you build compression in the leg and you can use that to spring off. That compression can help you take ground; think of the explosive forward movement in Xingyi's five fist postures.

Image D-8 shows me pushing off the rear leg and loading the lower back. I am taking the ground strength and moving it like a wave through the body. The Dantien is rolling up the back and then over the top in the next image (Image D-9). As I unfold, I shift into the front (right) kua and let the wave go through the arms into Colin.

Image D-9 – Releasing the wave through the arms sends Colin away.

I close into the right kua and the Dantien drops down the front as I shift my weight to my right leg (Image D-9). Colin has to take two or three steps to balance himself. The more speed you put into this, the more you will jolt your partner. Every movement in the internal arts contains this wave of internal strength, whether you notice it or not. As you develop skill, it becomes smaller.

The Power of Compression

"Sink your energy," is a common correction you will hear in an internal arts class. I was in a class being led by my teacher, Jim Criscimagna, and he asked us to do the Chen 19 form. When we were finished, he was not happy.

"Your chi is in your chest," he complained. He said we were carrying ourselves so high, we could not defend. We were weak.

"Sink your chi," he ordered. "Sink your energy."

Afterward, I muttered something to him, telling him that it was a good point about having our chi in our chest.

"Ahh, you weren't as bad as the others," he said.

Image D-10 below is an example of doing a movement from the Yang 24 form, "Part the Wild Horse's Mane," with your "chi in your chest." Image D-11 shows the same posture with my energy sunk. My chi is no longer in my chest.

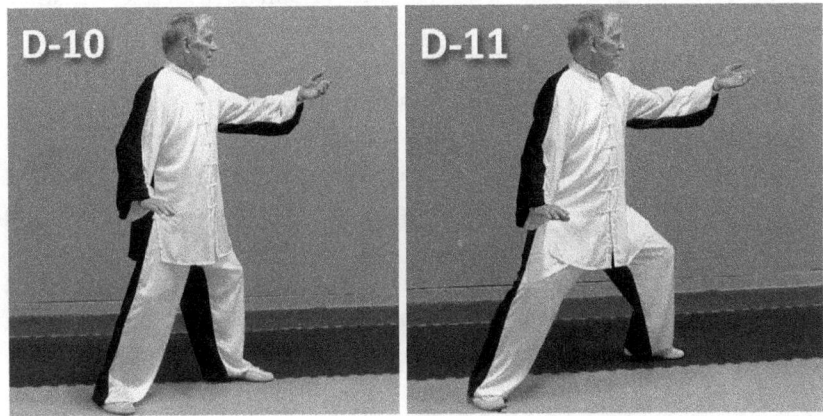

Image D-10 – "Part the Wild Horse's Mane" too high and shallow, with no sinking. Image D-11 – Dropping my energy and sinking more with a wider stance, closed a bit more into the left kua, with a rounded crotch instead of a "V."

Below are two more images showing a Bagua posture called "Push the Mountain" with my energy too high, then with my energy sunk.

Images D-12 and D-13 – Bagua's "Push the Mountain" with my chi in my chest and the same posture with chi sunk, sitting in my left kua, with ground path, peng jin, Dantien rotation – a solid stance.

Remember, just because I occasionally use the term "chi" in my teaching, that does not mean I believe chi is a scientific reality. However, it gives you a great mental visualization tool. I imagine energy coming into my body with the air I breathe, gathering and growing warmer in my Dantien. When I do qigong, I visualize it and feel it coursing through various pathways, depending on the exercise. I have even "felt things" as I have done qigong exercises.

But here is my logic: I can lie in bed at night, and if I am having a hard time sleeping, I close my eyes and visualize myself on a small boat, floating on a lake.

Within a minute or two, as I lie in my bed, I can feel the waves on the lake gently rocking the boat. It is very peaceful, just me in a boat, floating on a lake.

But when I open my eyes, the boat is not there. I am in a frikkin' bed, not in a boat. I felt the waves gently rocking me, but the waves did not exist. It was in my mind.

The same is true with chi. People swear they feel tingling and all types of things when they do qigong. I can do one qigong exercise and within a few seconds, I feel a ball of chi making a circle from my Dantien, through my arms and back to my Dantien again. That does not mean it is real. It means that the mind is a powerful tool, and we can use it to become better internal artists.

By keeping your chi (your energy; your weight) sunk, you will have stronger stances, stronger posture, and you will be better able to put all the key body mechanics together for Tai Chi, Xingyi and Bagua.

Sinking your energy means to relax your weight and let it drop. Flex the knees and relax the body. Feel your weight drop into the floor.

Sinking your energy and lowering your body a little has several advantages:

1. You are usually at an advantage when your center of gravity is lower than your opponent's.

2. You are more stable and able to generate more power.

3. By sinking your energy, you are better able to quickly deliver fajin, because you are already have compression. Just like the beach ball you push into the swimming pool, when you drop your weight, sinking your energy, you begin compressing, and the potential energy is waiting to spring out.

The internal arts are made up of openings and closings, store and release, compression and discharge, substantial and insubstantial, soft and hard. Using the body mechanics correctly helps achieve all these things.

Image D-14 – A beginning part of Xingyi's Splitting Palm (Pi Chuan), blocking forward.

Image D-15 – As I step forward to deliver the Splitting Palm, my lower back bows out because the Dantien is rotating under and to the back, then up the lower back. The right leg is compressing and I am preparing to spring off it and take ground with the left foot.

Image D-16 — The lower back unbows as the strike happens and the Dantien rotates over the top and forward with the palm strike.

Look at Images D-14 through D-16. As I step up and through with my left leg, the lower back bows out and unbows as the Dantien rotates with the store and release of the strike.

Like the bow and arrow, Image D-15 represents the bow being pulled back, creating the potential energy in the lower back. I am exaggerating for the photo to get the point across. There is compression in the right leg, also representing the storing of energy. There is a "closing" of the body, and the arms close together.

Image D-16 is the release of the energy with the Splitting Palm. The lower back unbows as the Dantien rotates violently forward, at the same time that I spring off the right foot and take ground. Notice my hips are under my body and I am in a centered stance as I strike. Image D-15 shows the closing of the body, while Image D-16 shows the opening of the body and the release of energy.

Depending on the movement and the application, the release of energy can also come in the closing of the body.

In Xingyi, the San Ti stance involves "loading" the rear leg (compression), and exploding off the leg to take ground and drive through your opponent. In Tai Chi and Bagua, too, there are countless instances of loading, storing, and releasing. Study each movement for yourself to find the openings and closings, and try to determine which represents storing and which represents the release.

It is worth repeating: there is nothing mystical about Dantien rotation. It is a physical skill that requires a lot of practice, and, to incorporate into every movement, it requires mental focus.

It literally takes years to get it down, but it also requires a lot of careful study, slow practice, and as much contemplation as a complex college course.

You do not learn all this as soon as you learn the choreography of a form. You may be able to remember all the moves, but it may be years before you can perform those moves at a high level of skill.

Your progress in the internal arts is not a race. You are training at your own pace. You will get it if you practice. But another important thing to remember is this: thinking about being skilled will not make you skilled. Only through practice, hard, boring, repetitive practice, does skill come.

We will see more about how the Dantien rotates when we put all the mechanics together in the Silk-Reeling Exercises later in the book.

6 MANIPULATING PENG AND WHOLE-BODY MOVEMENT

So far, we have studied how to establish the ground path, how to establish peng jin, how to open and close the kua, and how to rotate the Dantien. Next, we will look at ways of manipulating peng jin and the ground (the two are inseparable, remember) and how to start putting it all together with whole-body movement.

Exercise 8 – Down Energy

Image 8 – I exercise "down" energy while my partner uses "up" energy.

Up and down energy are generally taught together. We will start with down energy.

In Image 8 (previous page), my partner clenches his fists together and holds them in front of his body. I place my palms on top of his fists and relax my weight into his fists. In doing so, I am dropping my energy down; dropping my weight and using down energy.

At the same time, he is getting under the weight and supporting it with "up," or "supporting" energy.

When you work this with a partner, it is important that whoever is doing "down" energy does not use muscular force. They should not push down with their muscles. If they do, their partner needs to call them on it.

The proper way to do it is to put your intent in your hands and relax your weight into the hands..

Image 8-A – A common use for down energy – the arm bar. The more you let your weight provide the force, and not the muscle, the more "internal" you are.

Image 8-A shows a common use for down energy; the arm bar. Instead of forcing your opponent down with muscular power and brute force, put your intent into your forearm and drop your weight into his elbow. Other mechanics are also being used, but down energy is a key part. You see down energy all the time; in the dropping of the hands in the opening movements of Tai Chi, Xingyi and Bagua forms, and in movements throughout any internal form.

Exercise 9 – Up or "Supporting" Energy

Image 9 – I clench my fists and do "down" energy while Colin gets under it and supports it with "up" energy.

It is important to practice down and up energy. Images 8 and 9 show Colin using "up" energy by supporting my downward energy. He uses the ground path to the hands. To do this properly requires him to "get under" the downward weight. That often requires him to move his hips forward in a subtle way so he can get under it. This is something you will need to experiment with.

If you do not get under the downward energy well enough to support it with the ground, your hands will be too far in front, and the weight will feel as if it is forcing your arms downward. If you adjust your hips slightly, you will feel the weight in your hands connect with the ground, making it much easier to support.

It is important that neither you or your partner uses muscular force. The person doing downward energy relaxes his weight into his hands using intent. The person doing the supporting energy needs to get under it so the ground supports the weight in the hands. Do not press upward with your muscles to support the weight.

Supporting energy is used in many ways in martial arts. In Xingyi, for example, one of the self-defense applications of Tsuan Chuan (drilling fist) is to break your opponent's elbow with supporting energy if he grabs you by the shirt (see Image 9-A). Supporting energy can be found in applications throughout Xingyi, Tai Chi and Bagua forms. Upward palm in Bagua employs up, or supporting energy, in many of its applications. In all Tai Chi forms, you use up energy in the opening movement, as the arms rise in front of the body. If you are not visualizing and feeling the intent of getting under a weight as your arms rise in the opening movement, your Tai Chi is empty. Hint: you should *NOT* feel as if your arms are being lifted by strings. Your arms should be supporting a weight.

Image 9-A – Using Xingyi's Drilling Fist to break my opponent's elbow using "Up" or supporting energy.

When you do supporting energy, as in Image 9-A, it is powerless unless it is connected to the ground. And as this image demonstrates, the fist, or palm, is not always the primary point for striking in any of the internal arts. In this application, the ground is being put into the forearm, providing the power to break the opponent's elbow.

Look for ways to use down and up energy in all of your forms and techniques.

Exercise 10 – Whole-Body Movement

There is an interesting test to do on internal arts students and teachers to see if they know what they are doing.

Here is the test: you should stand like a teapot (or have someone else stand like a teapot) with one arm as the handle. See Image 10.

The person who stands like the teapot, with his arm like a handle, will be called "Person A." The person who is grabbing him will be known here as "Person B."

Image 10 – My partner stands with his arm like a handle. We call this the "teapot" posture. From the side, I grab his arm with my left hand.

I am Person B in these photos. You should ask your Person B to grab the handle of Person A. This means if Person A is standing as Colin is, with his left arm serving as the handle of the teapot, Person B will reach across with his left arm to grab the handle.

Now, you will ask Person B to pull Person A across Person B's body. I guarantee one of two things will happen with most internal arts students and teachers.

Image 10-A – Person B might turn the hips and let his arm lag behind.

If he is like a lot of people, Person B will turn his hips first, shift his weight, and leave his arm behind before he pulls and strains (Image 10-A). If he does this, that shows he is unaware of whole-body connection, and structural integrity is lost.

Image 10-B – Person B uses only arm muscle to pull.

The other major mistake people will do is to use only arm muscle to pull Person A, instead of using whole-body movement. Using "local" muscular power instead of whole-body movement is a sign that a person does not know internal body mechanics.

Internal artists love to talk about whole-body movement. They repeat sayings such as "When one part moves, all parts move; when one part stops, all parts stop." Finding people who can put it into practice is a different matter.

Whole-Body Connection

To have whole-body connection, strength begins with the ground. This means when I grab Colin, I set up a connection between the ground and my left hand. In Image 10, the ground path begins in the right foot, the one closest to Colin. There should be a tensile connection that I can feel between the right foot and the left hand.

As I begin to turn, I push from the ground, turn the waist and the arm as a single unit, and at the same time, I close the left kua and rotate the Dantien to the left. Remember to turn the waist, not the hips. All this happens at the same time as in the following images.

Image 10 – I establish the connection between the right foot and left hand.

Image 10-C – Connecting to the ground, turning the waist and arm together while closing into the left kua and rotating the Dantien to the left.

Image 10-D – Continuing to turn and close to the left, connected to the ground.

Image 10-E – Notice that I closed down and into the kua instead of sticking my left hip out to the side. I remained centered throughout.

If you study these four images, you will see that, like the beach ball in the swimming pool, I keep my structural integrity while throwing Colin away. And instead of kinking my hips and going off-balance to the left, I don't turn my hips very much; I turn my waist and close into the left kua. It is also crucial to turn the waist and arm together while connected to the ground.

Another mistake to watch for is the hip sticking out to the side. If you have someone do this exercise, watch the person who is doing the pulling. Notice that in the pictures, I pull across, but I am also moving down and into the left kua. A lot of people just move their hips across, and end up with their hips sticking out to the left.

Later in the book, you will be able to use whole-body movement when we go through some Silk-Reeling Exercises.

Exercise 11 – Manipulating Ground in 4 Directions

Learning to manipulate the ground path is another important skill. As you are practicing forms, as each movement is performed, you are constantly changing the focus of the ground path. When doing push hands, the ground path is constantly changing to adapt to your partner's changing force and position.

In this exercise, made up of four parts, a partner tests you by changing the direction of the force. Your job is to adapt to the change and maintain the ground path.

Image 11 – I clasp my hands together and hold them out as my partner presses straight in at me.

Image 11-A – My partner reaches over my clenched hands and pulls. I have to adjust the ground.

In these exercises, your partner is not applying hard pressure. These exercises do not make you Superman, they are intended to teach you important concepts. Naturally, if you are standing like this with your feet shoulder-width apart, you do not have a leg in front of you or behind you, so a hard push or a hard pull will cause you to move. That is not what this exercise is about, so the pull and the push should be just enough for you to test the ground, to feel the ground shifting.

When your partner pushes in, the ground will be more in your heels. When he pulls, it will shift to the bubbling well point and the balls of the feet.

Image 11-B – As my partner puts his weight in his hands with down energy, I get under it and support it.

Image 11-C – As my partner applies upward pressure to my fists, I sink my energy and use upward, supporting energy.

The next two are repeats of the up and down energies. Your partner will sink his weight into your fists (Image 11-B) and you will get under it and support it.

Next, he moves his hands under yours and applies upward pressure. Sink your energy into your fists to counter it (Image 11-C).

If your partner uses too much force in his push, call him on it. This exercise is not designed for someone to "win" if they push their partner off their spot. The person who is pushing needs to understand that this is a mutual learning situation.

As a variation, I also recommend standing with one leg out in front and one leg behind you. If you do, you will find it much easier to manipulate the ground.

In Tai Chi classics, they write that the "Yi leads the chi." In other words, the mind leads the chi.

If you ask a partner to stand with his fists in front of him, hands clasped together, and you tell him you are going to press into his fists so he can ground it, you will see something interesting. As you are moving to press into his hands, you will see his body adjust as he prepares for the push. By doing this subconsciously, he is demonstrating that his mind is leading his chi; in other words, he is setting up the ground path and peng jin to receive the push.

Exercise 12 – Grounding as Force Changes Direction

Another important skill is to manipulate the ground path as your opponent's force changes direction while he is touching you and moving. Your goal is to change directions with him and maintain the ground path and peng.

Image 12 – Colin pushes into my chest and I greet the push by establishing

In Image 12, Colin presses into my chest. I ground it to the left foot and establish a solid connection.

Image 12-A – Colin moves to my right, maintaining his push while I maintain the ground path, turning my waist with his movement.

Colin begins moving, forcing me to adjust my position. My goal is to maintain the ground path and peng without "breaking" as he moves. It is okay to pivot the feet, just pivot on the heels.

When doing any of these exercises, the person being pushed should realize when there is a "break" in his peng. Likewise, the person doing the pushing should "listen" very closely, and let his partner know if there is a break.

You know there is a break if you are pushing on someone, and it feels solid, then suddenly the solidity vanishes. It may only vanish for a split-second, but any break should be recognized.

When you are able to maintain and manipulate the ground path and peng jin, the person who is pushing should constantly feel as if they are pushing against something solid that is going from the point of contact into the ground. In Image 12, Colin should feel a solid connection as he pushes into my chest. When he moves and changes direction, he should not feel a break in that solidity.

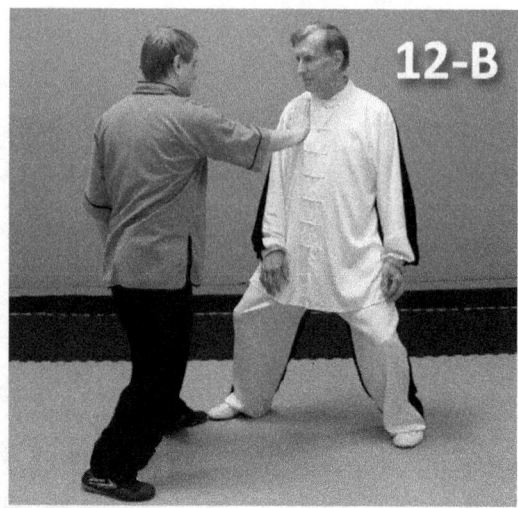

Image 12-B – Colin maintains his push and moves to my left, forcing me to follow his movement while maintaining ground and peng.

Colin keeps moving (Image 12-B), this time to his right (my left), causing me to turn my waist. If he continues moving to my left, I will change the grounding point from my left foot to my right foot.

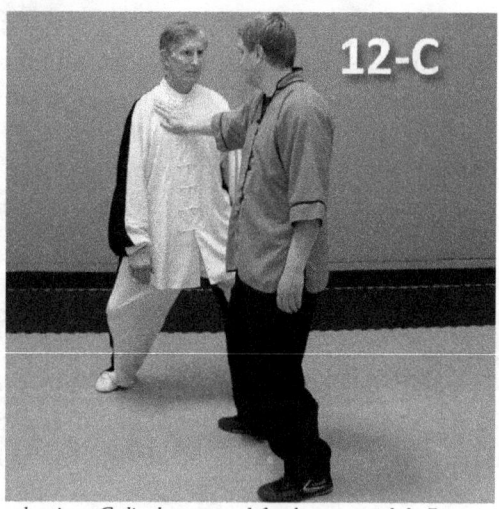

Image 12-C – By the time Colin has moved farther to my left, I am now grounding from the right foot. I am pivoting my feet as I follow him.

It is important to understand that this is merely an exercise to develop the ability to maintain ground and peng as the direction of the force changes. In a real-life self-defense situation, you will not stand in one position; you will move and change your position to adapt to your opponent.

As Colin continues to move to his right (my left), I switch the ground from the left to the right foot, but I do it without letting him feel a break. He should feel a solid ground connection as he pushes.

You can also do this exercise by extending your hand, letting your partner push into your extended palm as he moves around. Be creative and look for different ways of testing this skill. It sets up the next step in your internal development.

Exercise 13 – Maintaining Ground While Stepping

When I first learned of the ground path and peng, from Mike Sigman and Jim and Angela Criscimagna, I was curious about how in the world you can maintain the ground path as you stepped in an internal form or in self-defense.

It would seem that the ground connection would break if you took a step, right?

Not so fast, my young, silly friend. Relax your sphincter. This next exercise will answer that question.

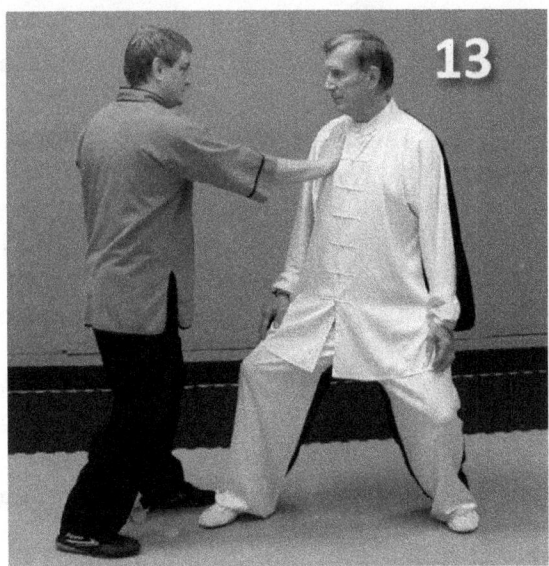

Image 13 – Colin applies steady pressure to my chest. I ground it to the left foot.

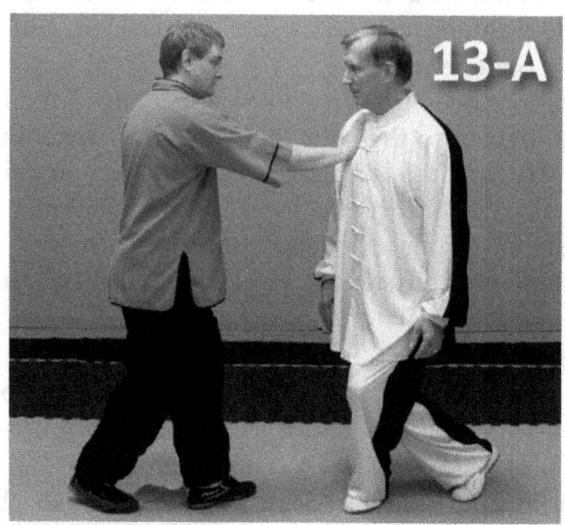

Image 13-A – I step forward with my left foot, switching the ground to the right foot as I step, but as soon as the left foot is planted, I ground from the left again.

I ground my partner's push from the chest to the left foot in Image 13, but as soon as I step forward and my left heel comes off the ground, I switch the ground to the right foot. I switch back to the left foot when it is planted in front of the right (Image 13-A), and I maintain the ground from the left foot as the right steps forward.

Colin's job is to maintain pressure, but not to prevent me from moving forward. He applies just enough pressure to check the ground path and make sure it does not break. He moves backward as I move forward, at the same speed, applying steady pressure.

Notice in the photos that I am keeping my body upright. I am not leaning forward or backward. I want to be as "centered" as I can be. When you are in a self-defense situation or in push hands, your opponent will be constantly trying to get the upper hand and to throw you off-balance, or worse.

Your goal is to always maintain your physical balance and your mental balance. By practicing the internal arts, you are always practicing to maintain both. So if you or your partner leans forward or backward or pushes too hard or uses too much muscle as they establish ground and peng, call them on it.

Image 13-B – My right foot has stepped forward. The ground is still in my left foot, but if I continue walking forward, I will switch to the right foot as soon as the left heel rises.

Another thing I would call your attention to is that my hips remain underneath me as I move. Do not let your butt stick out. Relax the lower back and let the buttocks drop. Some people might lead with their butt as they move forward or backward, but if you do not keep your hips under you, it is much harder to maintain the ground and peng.

You see, there is a reason we have these rules!

Exercise 14 – Grounding Against Joint Locks

If someone tries to put you into a joint lock, fighting against it with the ground path is not necessarily the choice I would make. Instead, I would use more advanced methods of going with the opponent's energy and spiraling out of it. That requires practice, and the ability to recognize a joint lock attempt before your opponent gets you firmly into the lock. Often, at that point, you are, as they say in gongfu, "screwed." I think that might be a Chinese term, but I am not sure.

However, this exercise is a good one to illustrate what ground strength can do.

Image 14 – My partner attempts an outside wrist twist. Step one is when he grabs my wrist as I attempt a punch or a push.

Image 14-A – As he attempts to twist my wrist to his left, I establish the ground path from my rear leg through my hand.

I punch or push toward my partner. To do an outside wrist twist, he grabs my right wrist with his left hand (Image 14).

He bends the wrist, grabs it with both hands and places his thumbs on the back of my hand, bending my hand at a 90-degree angle to my forearm.

As he begins to twist and torque my wrist, I establish the ground path from my rear leg through my hand and "extend" a little bit. The ground connection makes it very difficult for him to twist my wrist. If you practice this, be careful and experiment with the ground. Do not twist very hard at first, in case your partner is not good at this skill. You can gradually increase the force if you both agree, just be cautious because joint injuries are common if people are careless.

Image 14-B – Colin tries to put me in an arm bar, but I establish the ground connection from the left foot to the right elbow, making it very difficult for him to get the lock.

As you see in Image 14-B, you can try grounding against other types of locks, such as the arm bar. By establishing a ground connection and extending it through the joint that your partner is attempting to lock, it becomes extremely difficult for him to do the lock successfully.

A note of caution to make our lawyers happy: It does not take a rocket scientist to understand that joint locks can be dangerous, and so are punches and kicks and other strikes. It is very possible to be injured or injure a partner if both parties are not careful. Choose your partners carefully, and do not apply sudden, forceful pressure when practicing these techniques. You assume all liability for any injury that results. Nobody gets hurt in our practices. It is not necessary to injure anyone or to be injured yourself; you can become a good fighter without hurting anyone. So be careful. You could put your eye out, kid.

So far in this book, we have examined the ground path, peng jin, whole-body movement, Dantien rotation, and opening/closing the kua.

Next, as we practice Silk-Reeling Exercises, we put it all together.

7 SILK-REELING ENERGY
PUTTING THE MECHANICS TOGETHER

A few years ago, I wrote an eBook on Silk-Reeling energy (available on Kindle), and the introduction of the book was titled "Why You Do Not Understand Silk-Reeling Energy." A reviewer on Amazon said that I was arrogant.

I did not intend it as an arrogant statement about my knowledge. What I meant by that title, and the rest of the introduction, was how frustrated I am that there is so much mystical mumbo jumbo being taught about this skill. I had been a victim of the woo woo, too.

That sounds like a Dr. Seuss book title: "Are You the Victim of Woo Woo Too?" Or perhaps, "Master Brown Does Woo, Do You?"

But seriously, folks, the first time I was taught about Chan Ssu Jin (Silk-Reeling Energy), I was studying Yang style Tai Chi and I was told to "imagine" chi spiraling up through my leg, through my Dantien, through my torso, and out my hand. It was all about imagining chi. The only physical advice we were given was to press our foot into the ground. There was no instruction on ground path.

As I got into Chen Tai Chi, I learned that Silk-Reeling "energy" is not an actual energy inside the body, it is just another method of moving and dealing with force, like the other "energies" of Tai Chi (Ward Off, Roll Back, Press, Push, etc.).

Silk-Reeling is a physical skill that involves spiraling movement. When you combine it with the other body mechanics, the spiraling movement can add more impact and power to your movement, much like the beach ball that you jump on in the water spirals as it springs back. The spiraling gives the beach ball more power and leverage to dump you in the water.

Adding Silk-Reeling to your movement allows you to maintain your structural integrity and spin force away. It is a physical skill, not mystical or metaphysical.

Another Amazon reviewer said he liked my e-book on Silk-Reeling Energy, but he preferred to imagine chi in his mind rather than think of it as a physical skill. Think about that for a moment. He prefers the fantasy rather than the reality. And that, in a nutshell, is why Tai Chi is so ineffective as a martial art.

My friends, you can imagine chi until the day you die but you will not be effective. In my opinion, based on experience, that is the type of thing taught by teachers who have not had high-quality training.

Imagining chi will never give you the internal strength or relaxed power that comes from good structure and body mechanics.

In this chapter, I will describe how the body mechanics come together in more than a dozen Silk-Reeling exercises. There are more than 130 photographs in this section. I will try to break down the actual spiraling movement and body mechanics in detail. I recommend supplementing this information with the video in my Silk-Reeling Energy DVD, or you can also try a membership on my website (InternalFightingArts.com). The exercises here are sometimes numbered differently than in my DVD and eBook.

Silk-Reeling Exercise 1 – Single-Arm Reeling

Image 1-A – Starting position for Single-Arm Reeling.

In the first Silk-Reeling exercise, you stand with your feet wider than shoulder-width and your weight on your right leg. Your right arm is out. Your fingers can point straight up, as if you are gesturing someone to "Stop in the name of love!" Or, as in Image 1-A, your fingers can point a little more to the left. The ground is from the left foot.

One tip on most of these exercises is to make sure the hand is at least a little bit higher than the elbow. The left hand can rest on your left hip. You are into the right kua.

Image 1-B – Begin spiraling your hand, sinking your weight and dropping your arm.

Image 1-C – Your hand reaches your waist level. Your forearm and right hand are at a 90-degree angle.

Spiral the right hand down until it is at a 90-degree angle at the waist. Relax and sink a little deeper into the right kua. Notice from Image 1-A through Image 1-C, the hand is spiraling all the way. If you simply turn the palm outward at the top and drop it without spiraling it, that is a "dead spiral." Your hand should spiral continuously. When you are practicing with Grandmaster Chen Xiaowang, he calls the position in Image 1-C position "One."

Image 1-D – Ground from the right foot and begin spiraling the right hand to the middle. Your weight begins shifting to the middle and the waist turns with the arm.

Image 1-E – Your weight is more on the left and the hand is palm up almost at the centerline. Your waist (Dantien area) is facing forward.

Next, as shown in Image 1-D, you ground from the right foot and begin shifting to the left as your right hand begins to spiral to the middle of the body. The waist turns with the arm and you relax the left kua as your weight shifts. Open the right kua.

Not only is your hand spiraling, but as you move and shift your weight, the thighs are spiraling slightly, your Dantien is rotating to the right, your shoulder and elbow joints are spiraling, and make sure your hips are tucked and lower back is relaxed.

You are grounded as you shift your weight. If the only thing rotating is your hand, it is not quite right. This is whole-body movement, so you should be able to feel a subtle rotation in the legs, in the Dantien, and if someone grasped your shoulder or elbow, they should be able to feel a subtle spiraling of the joint.

Image 1-E shows position "Two." You have reached the center and the palm is facing up. The spiral from position "One" to position "Two" has been continuous. Make sure when you spiral, you don't stop spiraling until your hand reaches the centerline and your palm is facing up. If you stop the spiral too early, it is a "dead" spiral.

Although it may appear in Image 1-E that your weight is centered evenly on both legs, you are actually a bit heavier on the left leg than the right.

Image 1-F – Grounding from the right foot, begin spiraling your hand to the left, as if sweeping away a punch.

Image 1-G – Reaching the left side and position "Three."

Next, relax the left kua even more, ground from the right foot and spiral the right hand up and to the left, as if sweeping away a punch (Image 1-F). Your waist (not hips) and arm turn at the same time to the left. Do not collapse the right leg. Maintain peng in the legs.

In Image 1-G, you have reached Chen Xiaowang's position "Three."

Image 1-H – Begin shifting to the right and spiraling the hand across to the right. Ground from the left foot and turn the waist with the arm.

Image 1-I – Continue the spiral across the body, closing into the right kua.

Image 1-J – Position "Four," you are back where you started.

The last part of the exercise has you returning to the starting position. The ground shifts to the left foot and you relax the right kua, which starts the Dantien turning to the right (Image 1-H). The hand begins spiraling to the right as it crosses in front of your body. Your waist and arm turn together.

Image 1-J shows shifting and spiraling as it continues to the right, closing into the right kua with your weight reaching around 70% on the right leg by the time you reach position "Four" (Image 1-J).

After doing the right side as many times as you can, switch and do the same exercise with the left hand spiraling and the right hand resting on your side.

Important Tips for Exercise 1:
1. **Maintain the ground path at all times.** In Image 1-A, the ground is coming from the left foot. Beginning with Image 1-D, you are grounding from the right. Beginning with 1-H through 1-J, you are grounding from the left.
2. **Maintain peng jin at all times.** Notice the roundness in the arm and the way the legs do not collapse
3. **Spiraling happens throughout the body.** When the hand is spiraling, the legs are spiraling, the joints are spiraling, and even though it is so subtle that an untrained eye might not notice, it is happening. It is whole-body movement; when one part moves, all parts move; when one part stops, all parts stop.
4. **Spiral the hand all the way through the movement.** In each movement, you time the spiraling so it doesn't stop until the end of the section. For example, in Image 1-G through 1-J, you can see that the hand is spiraling all the way across, from the palm facing outward to the left (Image 1-G) to facing outward to the right (Image 1-J). It does not reach the outward position between 1-G and 1-J, it is spiraling that entire time.
5. **The waist turns with the arm and hand.** Turn the waist and arms as a single unit. Make sure you do not turn the waist first, letting the arms lag behind. And do not turn the arms without turning the waist. When the Dantien turns, the waist is generally turning.
6. **Keep the hips tucked. Do not let your butt stick out.**

When you become accustomed to all four parts of the first exercise, begin smoothing it out, but do not cut any section short. Even when doing the exercise smoothly, you should complete each section. For example, when doing the first part, let the hand come all the way down to waist level, then spiral across. Some people will cut that part short and begin moving the hand to the center before it reaches the low point in Image 1-C.

This is a great exercise that takes very little space. If you do it well, you are using the internal body mechanics and you are doing internal arts.

Silk-Reeling Exercise 2 – Double Arm Reeling

Image 2-A – Beginning posture for Double-Arm Reeling.

Double-Arm Reeling begins in the posture shown in Image 2-A, as if you are blocking a low kick, with your palms facing forward to the left, and 70% of your weight on your left leg. The ground from the right foot is directed into both hands. You are closed into the left kua; the right kua is open. Sink your weight into the floor. Your shoulders are level, the Dantien and waist are turned to the left. Peng is running through both legs. Your "intent" is in your hands as if blocking a low kick.

Image 2-B – "Get under" and begin spiraling the arms up.

Next, you adjust your lower body as if "getting under" a weight, and you begin spiraling the arms upward (Image 2-B). I visualize someone punching at me and I am moving to intercept the punch. Your weight is still 70% on the right leg.

Image 2-C – You have spiraled your arms up as if intercepting a punch.

In Image 2-C, your hands reach the top of the spiral, and are in a posture that works if you try to intercept or "catch" an incoming punch. Imagine your right hand grabbing a wrist and the left hand connecting at the elbow or triceps. If you were practicing this with Chen Xiaowang, he would say this is position one.

Image 2-D – Grounding from the left foot and "pulling" to the right.

Next, you switch the ground from the right to the left foot and you "pull" the arm that is throwing the punch you have just intercepted. You are pulling toward the right leg. Your arms spiral as you close into the right kua and turn the Dantien and the waist to the right with the arms. Maintain peng through the arms and legs and the shoulders remain level.

You are not just spiraling in the arms. Your legs are spiraling very slightly, your Dantien is rotating horizontally from left to right. Your shoulders and elbows are spiraling. And as your hands spiral across, make sure they are spiraling the entire time. You don't reach the end of the spiral until your hands stop when they get to the right side.

One application of this is easy to visualize. You have stepped in front of your opponent, caught his punch, and now you are pulling him over your leg in a takedown.

I demonstrate this starting on page 109.

Image 2-E – Reaching the end of the spiral to the right side, what Chen Xiaowang would call position "two."

Image 2-E shows me reaching position "two," the end of the spiraling to the right. I have closed into the right kua, the Dantien is turned to the right and the ground is coming from the left foot.

Image 2-F – Start spiraling and sinking the weight downward.

Next, begin spiraling the hands downward as you sink your "energy" (your weight) and close down a bit more into the right kua. Your intent is to put downward energy, or put the intent of your weight, into your hands.

Image 2-G – Reaching the bottom of the spiral, position "three."

At the bottom of the spiral (Image 2-G), you really sit into the kua. You can think of this as the end of an armbar takedown, with "downward," relaxed energy in your hands. Notice the peng in both legs; no straightening out and locking the knees. Chen Xiaowang would call this position "three."

Image 2-H – Beginning the shift and the spiral back to the original position to the left.

Now, you begin shifting your weight back to the left. You relax the left hip, which starts the "sit back" movement to the left, and it causes your Dantien to begin moving left. Pushing the ground from the right foot, your hands spiral as your Dantien and waist turn left. The entire body is spiraling slightly, including the legs.

Remember, videotape yourself or get a trained eye to watch you to make sure your hands are actually spiraling the entire way across the body. If the spiral is not continuous, keep working on it.

Image 2-I – Reaching the original position to the left, as if blocking a kick.

When you reach the end of the four-movement cycle, you will be back where you began, with your weight shifted to the left foot, in the left kua, with your hands down as if blocking a low kick (Image 2-I). The ground is coming from the right foot and you have peng through the arms and the legs. The waist is turned to the left. The hips are not turned as much as the waist. The hips should be facing basically in the same direction as the feet.

Chen Xiaowang would call this position "four."

Keep repeating the cycle. Do not cut any of the parts short. It is common for beginners to not complete the four postures that you see here at One, Two, Three and Four. Sometimes, you will be tempted to speed up and not quite be as strict as these pictures show.

It is important to work on gradually doing it smoothly, not really stopping completely at each position, but just make sure you hit each point as you get a little faster and smoother, maintaining the body mechanics and the spiraling the entire way.

You are putting the six body mechanics to work now.

Image 2-J – Colin punches and I move to intercept the punch.

Just as there are many self-defense applications possible for each movement in Xingyi, Tai Chi and Bagua, there are also several applications possible for each of the silk-reeling exercises.

Here is one application of this silk-reeling exercise. Colin punches at me and I move to intercept his punch (Image 2-J).

Image 2-K – I grab his wrist and just above the elbow and step in front of his leg.

Image 2-L – By blocking his leg with mine, I create leverage.

Image 2-M – I pull across and Colin falls to the mat.

Look at the sequence carefully – Images 2-J through 2-M. I step in front of Colin and my left leg seals his right leg. Our legs are pressed together, my calf to his shin. Be sure to step in close enough. You have to get up-close and personal.

In Image 2-L, I ground from the left foot to my hands and my waist (Dantien) and my hands move across together. It is a whole-body, coordinated movement. The hands are connected to the Dantien which is connected to the ground.

Notice in Image 2-M just how much my stomach/waist has moved but how little my hips have moved. If I kinked my hips by turning them to the right with my hands, my structure would not have been solid and my whole-body connection would have broken. In Image 2-M, you can see that my frog buttons are turned to the right even more than they are in Image 2-L, but the hips are in the same place.

Also, notice my arms are not collapsing. There is peng throughout the application. And look at the legs. When I turn Colin, my front leg does not collapse. When you watch videos of Tai Chi people in the future, watch to see how often their knees collapse. Some of them regularly lose the peng in their legs.

I am not dealing with self-defense applications for most of the exercises in this book. That is for further study, but it is important for you to get a glimpse of how the body mechanics work when you put them all together.

The author with Chen Xiaowang at a Silk-Reeling workshop in 2000.

Silk-Reeling Exercise 3 – Up/Down Diagonal Arms

This exercise helps you use spiraling in two diagonal directions. Similar movements can be found in Tai Chi, Xingyi and Bagua.

Image 3-A – Start with your hands at up and down angles.

Exercise three begins with a posture as shown in Image 3-A. Your palms face away from you and your arms are at up and down angles.

In this image, my weight is on my right leg and my main focus is in the right hand. I am closed into the right kua and I have intent in both hands. The ground for the right hand is from the left foot; the ground for the left hand is from the right foot.

Image 3-B – The hands begin spiraling as I sit into the right kua.

Begin spiraling the hands and sinking deeper into the kua as in Image 3-B. Close the obliques on the right side as you open the obliques on the left side. Your energy drops on the right and rises on the left, but the hips remain level. The right hand spirals down and the left hand spirals up.

Image 3-C – Begin shifting to the left as the hands keep spiraling.

Your right hand spirals inward, powered by the ground from the right foot (Image 3-C). Relax the left kua and the waist turns with the right hand as your weight shifts to the left.

Image 3-D – Reaching the end of the shift to the left. The hands are ready to spiral at angles again.

Keep spiraling the hands as you close into the left kua and turn the waist to the left, reaching the end of the shift to the left (Image 3-D).

Image 3-E – Begin shifting to the right and spiraling the hands at angles.

Relax the right kua and spiral the hands at angles as you "sit back" and begin shifting to the right (Image 3-E). Maintain intent in both hands. The ground for the right hand is coming from the left foot, and the ground for the left hand is coming from the right.

There is a slight "sitting back" toward the right as you begin this movement. That often implies a shoulder strike.

Image 3-F – Continue shifting to the right and spiraling the hands.

You can easily see the elbow strike in Image 3-F. Continue shifting to the right and spiraling the hands; the right hand is spiraling up at an angle and the left is spiraling downward, as if blocking a low kick. There are several applications for each of the silk-reeling exercises, just as there are when these movements are used in Xingyi, Tai Chi and Bagua forms.

Notice the peng that is present throughout the body, through the legs and the arms. My body is straight, head is up and shoulders level. As a beginner, you might tend at this point to lock the left knee or collapse it as you shift to the right, but that puts you in a vulnerable position.

Another application for this movement, as you can perhaps see in Image 3-G, is a palm strike to the face with the right hand as you pull down the opponent's punching hand with your left hand.

You can see more demonstrations of applications in the videos through the course at www.InternalBodyMechanics.com.

Image 3-G – Your spirals reach the end, returning to the original position.

After returning to the original posture (Image 3-G), repeat the sequence. Smooth out the sinking, the spiraling, and relaxing and closing/opening of the kua, shifting the weight, turning the Dantien and maintaining ground, peng and intent.

As with all of these exercises, after practicing with the right hand going up at an angle, switch sides and practice with the left hand angling upward.

Silk-Reeling Exercise 4 – Inward Reeling

Image 4-A – Start on the left side, left palm up and right palm down.

The Inward Reeling exercise focuses the spiraling on the elbows. In Image 4-A, you begin with your weight on the left side, with forearms at angles upward, left palm facing upward and right palm facing downward. You are closed into the left kua.

Image 4-B – Begin shifting to the right as the left elbow spirals inward.

Relax the right kua and begin shifting your weight to the right leg. The left elbow will begin spiraling inward and the right elbow will move downward to the right. The ground path begins with the left foot and can be expressed both in the left and right elbows.

Image 4-C – Right elbow begins to rise, left begins to drop.

The left elbow spirals toward the centerline, then begins to spiral downward, and the right elbow begins rising on the right (Image 4-C). To the untrained eye, it might appear that you are moving your hands in circles, but the focus of the spiraling is in the elbows.

At this point, you are sitting into the right kua and the waist is turning right. Ground is still from the left foot.

Image 4-D – Right elbow still rising as the left elbow spirals down.

In Image 4-D, your right elbow is rising and almost ready to spiral inward, while the left elbow is starting to spiral downward. The energy on the right side of the body is rising while the left side is dropping. You are now shifting the ground to the right foot.

Image 4-E – The right elbow spirals inward, left elbow outward.

Relax the left kua as the right elbow begins spiraling inward, across the body, and the left elbow spirals outward (Image 4-E). You "sit back" and begin to shift to the left side and the Dantien and waist turn to the left with the elbows. The ground path is starting from the right foot. Notice that the hips and shoulders remain level.

Image 4-F – Weight on the left, left arm rises and right elbow spirals down.

Image 4-G – Back to the original position, ready to repeat the exercise.

As Images 4-F and 4-G show, your right elbow reaches the centerline and begins to spiral downward, as the left elbow rises and is prepared, in Image 4-G, to begin spiraling inward. Repeat the exercise as many times as you want. This exercise works both sides of the body, so there is no need to "switch sides" as you do some of the other exercises.

This movement of spiraling the elbows is seen in movements and self-defense applications involving elbow strikes, deflections and more.

It is important that your arms remain relaxed, but with internal strength, throughout the spiraling movements. Also, as in all the exercises, your movement should be connected throughout the body, from the feet to the hands, with all parts moving together.

Silk-Reeling Exercise 5 – Push Out/Pull Down

This exercise focuses on moving the internal strength in a "wave" through the lower back and torso, then exercises whole-body movement in pulling down. Think of it as grasping an opponent's lapels and "plucking" him downward.

Image 5-A – Start on your right side as if pushing someone.

This exercise involves silk-reeling plus a pull-down that can be used forcefully to "pluck" someone to the ground, although the exercise is practiced slowly so you can master the body mechanics.

Begin on either side. In Image 5-A, I begin on the right side. I have relaxed the right kua, my weight is on the right foot, and my hands are out as if I have just pushed someone. The ground is coming from the left foot. Hips and shoulders are level, and there is peng throughout the body. The waist is turned to the right.

Image 5-B – Sink the weight as you relax the kua.
The hands begin closing into fists as they drop slightly.

Next, you sink the weight and drop the Dantien (Image 5-B). Your hands lower slightly as they begin to form into fists.

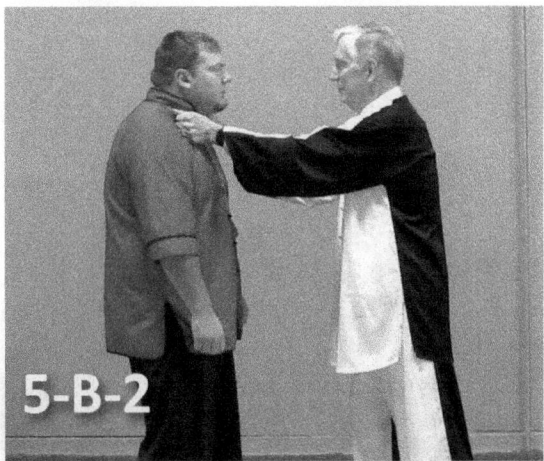

Image 5-B-2 – The fighting application of Image 5-B.

The actions in Images 5-B, 5-C and 5-D cam be used to unbalance an opponent in front of you. By grabbing your opponent's lapel, you can put him off-balance forward or backward using the action in Images 5-C and 5-D.

Image 5-C – The hands form fists as they coil and ground rises from the left foot.

In this exercise, the Dantien drops and rotates to the back, up the back, and then down the front again, in a vertical "over the top" circle. In Image 5-C, as the hands form fists and begin to coil toward you, the Dantien rotates under and backward. The lower back begins to bow out, like an archer pulling back the string.

Image 5-B-2 – Curling the wrists and bringing your hands in while sinking your weight causes even a large man like Justin to lean in. He weighs 110 pounds more than I do.

Image 5-D – Your fists have rotated over and the Dantien has rotated back to the front.

The fists rotate over the top, the lower back unbows as the Dantien rotates over and to the front, the ground path coming from the left foot. The internal power can be seen as a "wave" traveling up the leg, through the lower back, through the shoulders, arms, and fists. This movement is as if you have grabbed your opponent by the lapels and rotated your fists down and over in a circular motion to unbalance him backward.

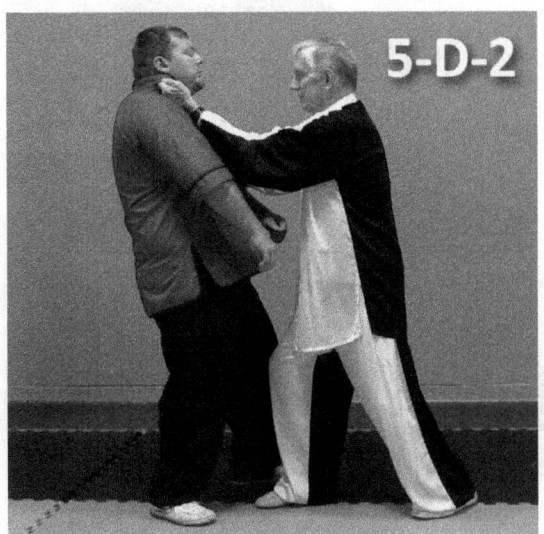

Image 5-D-2 – By rolling my fists outward, using whole-body movement and grounding to my rear foot, Justin is forced off-balance backward.

The action of the lower back bowing and unbowing is a lot like the archer, pulling back the string of his bow (bowing out--convex) and then releasing it (unbowing--concave).

When you perform this exercise, your back bows and unbows more slowly, because the exercise helps you master the body mechanics. Later, when working it as a fighting application, you can "turn on the gas," as Chen Xiaowang would say, adding speed and power to the movement.

This movement is as if you have grabbed your opponent by the lapels and rotated your fists down and over in a circular motion to unbalance him.

Image 5-E – Grounding from the right foot, begin pulling your opponent down.

Next, as seen in Image 5-E, you ground from the right foot and drop your energy, sitting deeply into the right kua and using your dropping weight to help pull down your opponent.

Image 5-F – Turning the waist and arms as one unit, pull your fists across your body.

Connecting to the ground from the right foot, relax the left kua and rotate the Dantien to the left, pulling your fists across to the left and turning the waist with the fists.

Image 5-G – Closing into the left kua and the fists reach the left leg and begin to open again.

After pulling the fists across to the left, you have closed into the left kua and your waist is turned to the left (Image 5-G). You are now preparing to "sit back" as you relax the right kua. Do you notice how the waist has turned, but the hips have not turned too far to the left?

Image 5-H – Open the hands and sit back into the right kua as you begin turning to the right.

Relax the right kua, sit back and open the fists as you begin turning the waist and the hands to the right, connecting with the ground from the left foot (Image 5-H). The lower back is filling up.

Image 5-I – Push with both hands to the right, ending in the original posture.

You push the hands out in an unfolding motion from the left to the right. As you turn from left to right, between images 5-H and 5-I, the lower back bows out and then, as you reach the right side and push, the lower back unbows. The ground connects from the left foot to the hands. You have closed into the right kua. As the hands push out, the Dantien drops down as your weight settles.

Continue and repeat the exercise as many times as you want, then switch sides, beginning by pushing out to the left.

It is not easy to capture the "wave" that happens through the body in photos. It is easier to demonstrate on video.

Silk-Reeling Exercise 6 – Small Arm Spiral

The Small Arm Spiral is a lot like Silk-Reeling Exercise #1, but it is in a much smaller form. When speeded up, the coiling through the arm, wrist and hand is very obvious.

The spiraling action is commonly seen in movements such as the initial blocking action of Xingyi's Drilling Fist, the initial coiling of the hands in Chen Tai Chi's Six Sealings Four Closings movement (the Xinjia version), and in many movements of Bagua.

Image 6-A – Start with your weight on the right leg and right palm extended.

Begin by standing with your right palm extended and your weight on the right leg. The left hand can be hanging or at your waist as shown in Image 6-A. Dantien is turned slightly to the right.

Image 6-B – Begin by sinking the energy and dropping the right hand.

Sink, sit deeper into the right kua as your hand drops downward slightly. Like other movements involving the dropping of energy, your right-side obliques will close and you will feel the pressure of dropping increase in the right leg. The Dantien will settle downward.

Image 6-C – Pull the hand inward as Dantien turns to the right.

Next, relax the left kua. The Dantien turns slightly to the left and the hand spirals slightly to the left (Image 6-C), using the ground from the right foot. You feel the compression building in the left foot like pressure of the beach ball pushed into the water.

Image 6-D – Supporting energy as the right hand spirals upward.

Using the ground from the right foot for support, spiral the right hand so the palm is upward (Image 6-D). The Dantien will be rotating upward at this point.

Image 6-E – As the hand reaches the top of the spiral, it begins to spiral so the palm will face outward.

The ground is shifted to the left foot as the hand spirals and the palm begins to turn outward (Image 6-E), the Dantien is rotating to the right and you are relaxing the right kua.

Image 6-F – The palm faces outward and the end of the spiral.

At the end of the spiral (Image 6-F), your palm will face outward and your stance will be similar to Image 6-A, the beginning of the exercise. There is a difference in how the palm is facing. At the end of the exercise, you can visualize a situation where you are grabbing the wrist of an opponent's incoming punch.

The ground path is from the left foot to the right hand in Image 6-F, and you are closed into the right kua.

Repeat the exercise as many times as you want, then switch to the left side and the left hand.

Here is a close-up view of this exercise from a different angle.

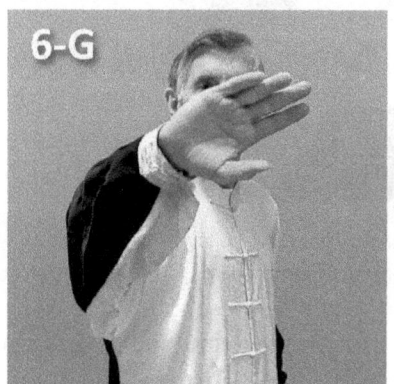
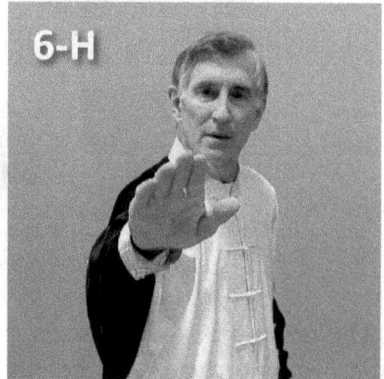
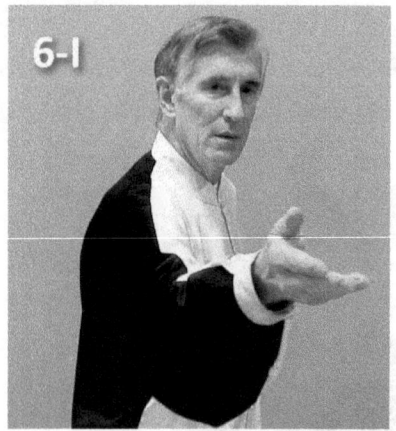

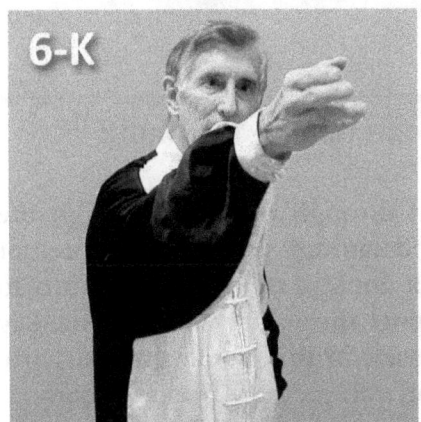 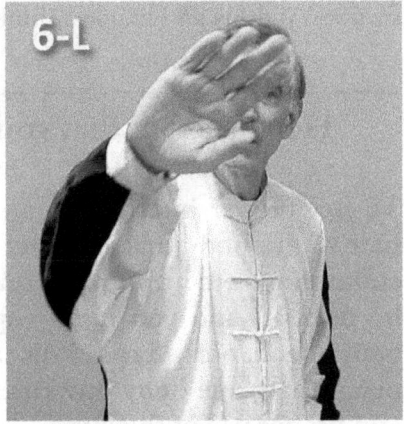

Images 6-G through 6-L – A close-up view of Small Arm Spiral.

It is important to maintain a relaxed wrist when doing this exercise. Men are often raised to avoid a "limp wrist." It has always been identified with feminine traits. But in Tai Chi, you must loosen your wrists and joints, and avoid being stiff.

One good way to begin relaxing the wrist is to imagine your hand is a paint brush; the palm and fingers are the bristles. Moving your arm side to side causes your hand and fingers to bend back and forth, like the bristles of a paint brush. Your wrists must be loose and relaxed to accomplish this.

Your shoulder and elbow joints must also be relaxed. Remember, the internal power comes from the ground, transmits up the legs, directed by the Dantien, and travels on through the torso, shoulders, elbows and hands. The kua helps coordinate internal power from the legs to the torso. What these photos do not show well is the spiraling through the arm, and how smooth it all looks at higher speeds.

Challenge Alert -- This exercise shows a clockwise rotation of the hand. Your challenge now is to practice in this direction, then change directions and spiral the hand counter-clockwise.

Silk-Reeling Exercise 7 – Single Shoulder Spiral

You may hear talk in the internal arts about opening the joints, and you may read articles by internal artists who talk about transmitting chi through the joints. This is interpreted different ways, from fantasy to reality. In this book, we remain firmly rooted to the ground, all our structure and movement guided by solid internal principles, not mystical visions and magical thinking.

Here is a fact that you can take to the bank:

To get proper internal strength through the joints and to the part of the body that is either "listening" to incoming force or countering force, you must relax enough to allow your joints to be flexible, and you must support the joints with the six key body mechanics that are discussed in this book: ground path, peng jin, whole-body movement, silk-reeling, Dantien rotation, and proper use of the kua.

This next Silk-Reeling exercise isolates the shoulder joint, using the ground and a shifting of weight to spiral the shoulder in two directions.

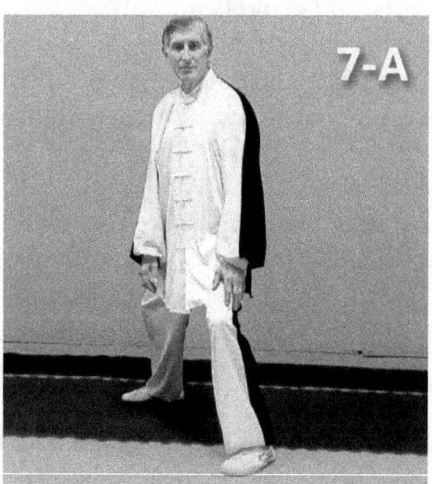

Image 7-A – Stand with your weight on your forward foot (left foot in this image) and your left shoulder relaxed and forward.

Begin by standing with one leg forward. In this exercise, we will start with the left leg forward. Relax the left kua and relax the shoulders and the arms. As you begin, as in Image 7-A, the ground path is coming from the rear foot.

The images on the next few pages are sometimes larger than usual so you can more clearly see the spiraling movement.

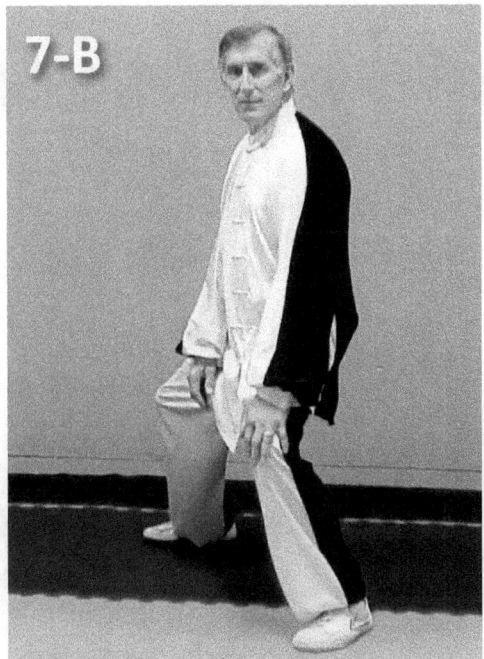

Image 7-B – Sit into the left kua and move the shoulder forward as it begins a circle. T

You are going to isolate and circle the left shoulder to the front of your body and then to the back.

Start spiraling, as in Image 7-B, by sitting into your left kua and moving the left shoulder forward. The ground comes from the rear foot. The left arm is completely relaxed, so the left hand will move with the movement of the shoulder.

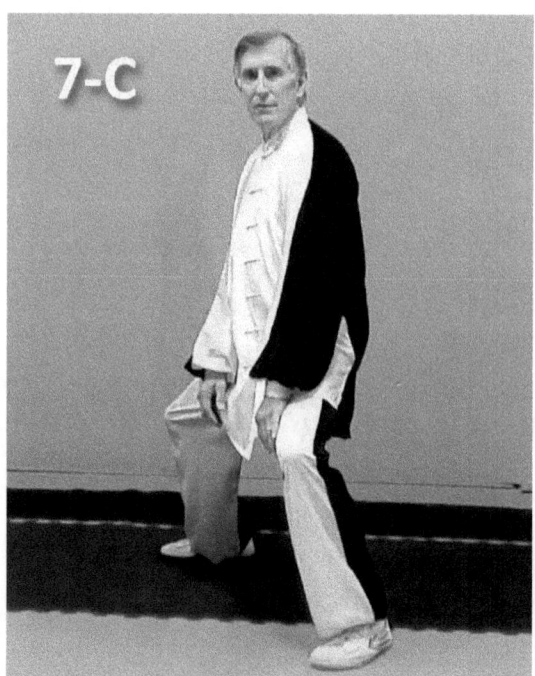

Image 7-C – With the ground coming from the front foot, begin moving as a unit and circling the shoulder to the inside of the body and upward.

Next, you switch the ground to the front foot, relax the right kua and begin sitting back as the shoulder circles to the front of the body. You are connected to the front foot. The Dantien is rotating to the right. The waist is not turned very much in this exercise, but as always, the Dantien is rotating. The hips hardly turn at all.

It is important not to use the arm muscles in this exercise. You are isolating the shoulder.

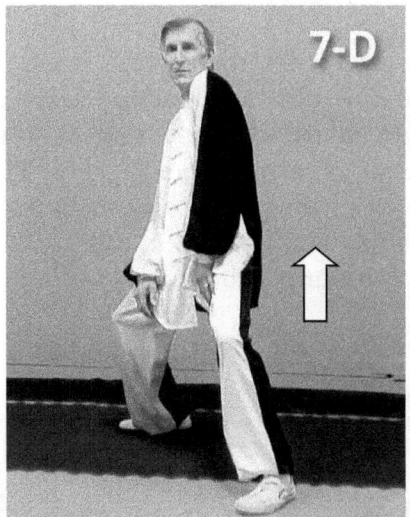

Image 7-D – Closing into the right kua, the left shoulder circle reaches the top, as if protecting your chin from a strike.

Continuing to connect with the ground from the left foot, you will sit back into your right kua as the shoulder reaches the top of its circle. At this point, from a self-defense perspective, the shoulder is protecting your jaw from a strike.

The Dantien rotation is up the left side, as indicated by the arrow.

Image 7-E – Rotate the shoulder to the back.

The Dantien now rotates to the left, toward the back, as the shoulder also rotates past the head and to the backside. You are now transitioning the ground path from the front foot to the rear foot.

Your waist doesn't move much here, and the hips are not turning, but the Dantien is rotating with the shoulder. It is an internal movement. The lifting and rotating of the shoulder might make it appear that the body is turning, but it is not.

Image 7-F – The rotation of the shoulder continues.

The shoulder continues rotating to the left. It will begin dropping as it rotates toward the front again, and the Dantien will rotate with it. The ground is now being connected through the rear foot.

Image 7-G – Continuing the circle of the shoulder toward the starting position.

In Image 7-G, your shoulder continues to spiral down and to the front. The Dantien is also moving down and to the front with the shoulder. You return to the original position (Image 7-H). You can continue spiraling in the same direction or change directions, as we demonstrate in the next sequence of photos.

Image 7-H – Back to the start. From here, you can spiral in either direction.

Changing Directions with Single Shoulder Spiral

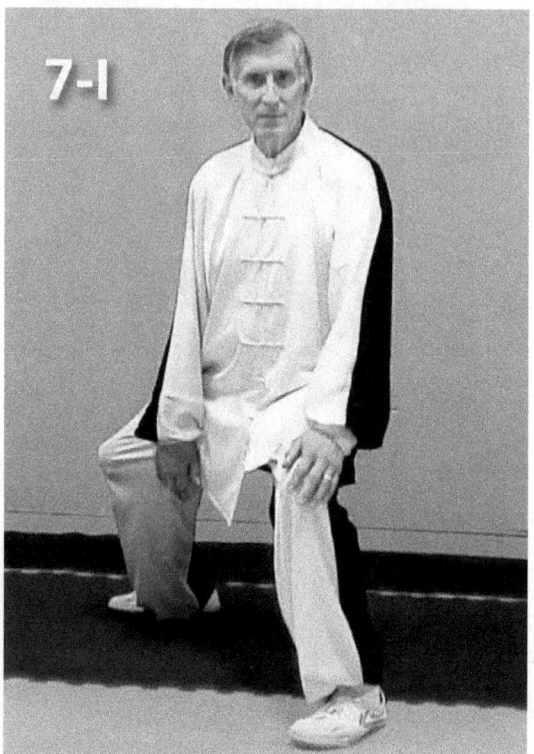

Image 7-I – Spiral the shoulder in the opposite direction, up the backside.

To spiral in the opposite direction, connect the shoulder to the ground in the front foot and spiral it to the left, to the backside, and up toward the head. The Dantien should rotate with it. Your weight begins to shift toward the rear leg.

Image 7-J – Ground from the left foot to the shoulder as it spirals up and back..

The Dantien rotates upward as the shoulder nears the head (Image 7-J). The ground is still connected from the front (left) foot. You are into the right kua and more of your weight is on the right leg.

Image 7-K – Rotate the shoulder across toward the front of the body.

At the top of the circle, rotate the shoulder across, as if protecting the jaw from a strike (Image 7-K). The Dantien rotates to the front, guiding the shoulder, and you are into the right kua (left kua is open). Pressure is building on the right leg, like the beach ball being pressed into the pool.

Image 7-L and 7-M – Shoulder spirals back to starting position forward.

The shoulder begins to drop down (Image 7-L), with the Dantien guiding it, as it rotates toward the starting position. You sit a bit more into your right kua and the ground comes from the rear foot, but you are preparing to move back toward the left kua.

When you return to the original position (Image 7-M), you can continue the same direction or change directions whenever you want.

When you have had enough rotating the left shoulder, change positions and rotate the right shoulder.

This exercise, and the resulting flexibility it gives your shoulders, has a variety of uses in both internal movement and self-defense.

Silk-Reeling Exercise 8 – Double Shoulder Spiral

The Double Shoulder Spiral is double the fun of the Single Shoulder Spiral. The internal strength flows like a wave from the feet, through the shoulders, and back to the feet again. The purpose is to relax the shoulders, isolate them for various self-defense applications, and coordinate their spiraling with whole-body movement.

Start by standing in a stance similar to the Single Shoulder Spiral, but with both arms hanging at your sides and your torso facing forward (Image 8-A).

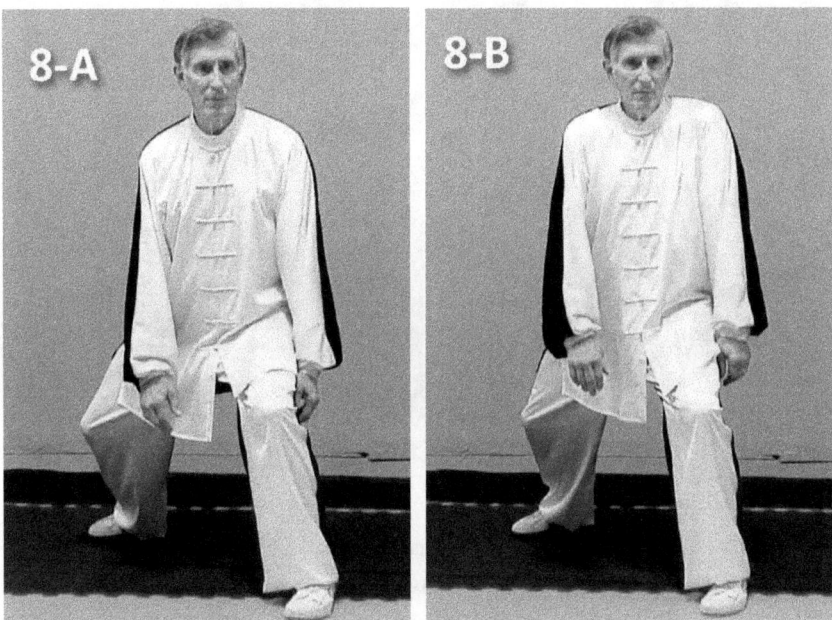

Image 8-A – Stand and let arms hang at your sides. Image 8-B – Begin spiraling the shoulders up and back.

Connecting to the ground from the front foot (left foot in these images) to the shoulders, relax the right kua and begin sitting back as the shoulders both start to spiral backward (Image 8-B). The Dantien will spiral in a vertical circle back and over-the-top. Let the arms hang.

Image 8-C and 8-D – Rolling the Shoulders Back and then Down.

In Image 8-C, the shoulders and the Dantien, both spiraling together and connected to the ground via the front foot, reach the top of their spiral. Close into the right kua and open the left kua.

The shoulders and Dantien both continue their spiral down the backside. You begin sinking more into the right kua, compressing the right leg and beginning to shift the ground path to the right foot.

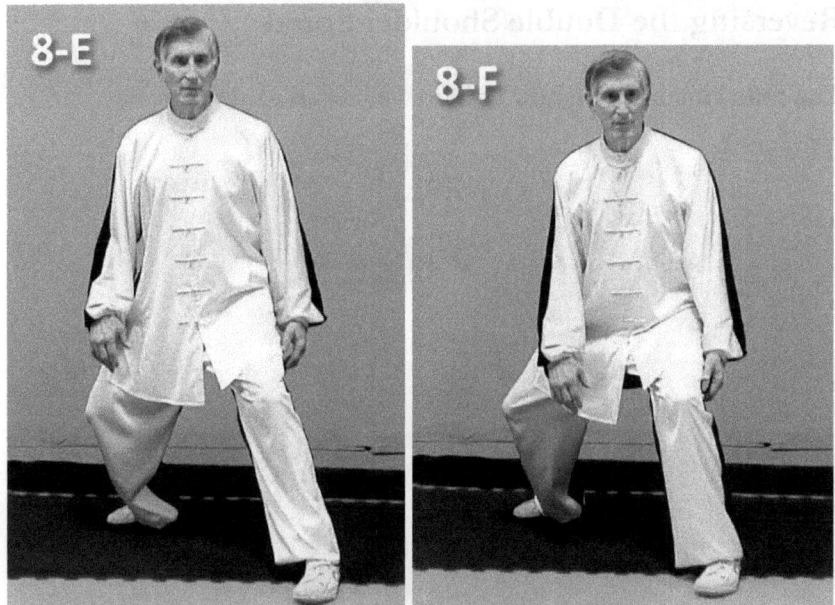

Image 8-E – The shoulders and Dantien reach the bottom of the spiral.
Image 8-F – Push the ground from the right foot and bring the shoulders forward.

In Image 8-E, the bottom of the spiral. Sit into the right kua as the shoulders and Dantien reach the bottom. The ground path is firmly established in the right foot.

Connecting to the ground from the right foot, continue the rotation of the shoulders and Dantien forward and sit into the left kua (Image 8-F).

Now, you are ready to continue the sequence and do it again. Do it continuously, and then change directions.

Reversing the Double Shoulder Spiral

The following images show you how to reverse this exercise.

Image 8-G – Relax the right kua and begin spiraling the shoulders down and back.

Connecting the ground through the left (front) foot, relax the right kua, "sit back" and begin spiraling the Dantien and shoulders to the rear (Image 8-G)

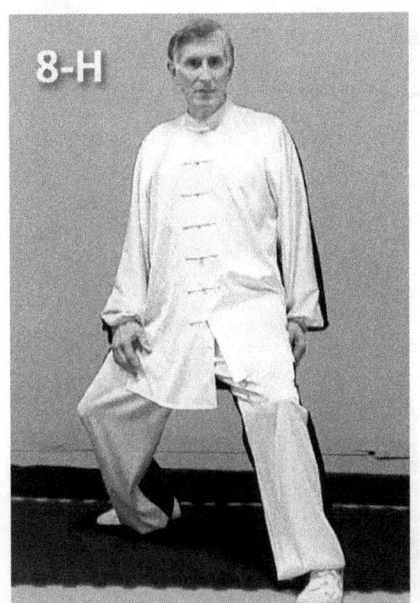 

Image 8-H – Shoulders reach the back and begin rising in Image 8-I.

You see in Image 8-H that the shoulders are relaxed and connecting to the ground through the front foot. Sit back into the right kua and move your shoulders toward the back. Important note: keep your body straight. Do not lean backward. You want your energy and intent to be forward. The Dantien rotates down and back, in an opposite circle compared to the last exercise.

When your shoulders go back as far as they can, you have compressed and connected the right leg and are ready now to switch the ground path to the rear leg.

Next, rotate the shoulders upward, as if shrugging (Image 8-I). The ground path is connected from the rear foot to the shoulders, and the Dantien is also rotating upward, bowing out the lower back as it goes in a wave up the body.

Image 8-J – Rotate the shoulders toward the front.

Continue with the forward circle by rotating the shoulders from the back to the front as you close into the left kua (Image 8-J). The ground is still connecting from the rear leg and the Dantien is rotating from top to front. The lower back, after bowing out during the rising of the Dantien, is now beginning to unbow as the Dantien rotates forward.

Return to the original posture; into the left kua, arms hanging at your sides, and shoulders pushed a bit forward (Image 8-K). The ground path comes from the rear leg and the Dantien has dropped to the front.

At this point, you can continue the same spiraling sequence or reverse the direction.

Silk-Reeling Exercise 9 – Diving Palm Spiral

The Diving Palm Spiral is a common spiraling movement in Baguazhang. Like the other silk-reeling exercises, you are working all of the body mechanics for good internal gongfu.

Image 9-A – Begin with palm extended and facing up.

Begin by standing with your weight on the right leg, closed into the right kua and right arm extended with palm up (Image 9-A). Ground path extends from the left foot to the right hand. The Dantien is turned to the right. The left hand can be held at your side or resting on your side, as shown.

Image 9-B – Bring the hand back toward the head as you sit back.

Connect the ground between the right foot and the right forearm and relax the left kua. As your weight shifts to the left, your hand is drawn back toward your face as if your fingers are going to poke you in the eyes. The Dantien is rotating over the top and to the left.

Image 9-C – Curl the hand under as you sit deeper into the left kua.

In Image 9-C, you start curling the right hand under as you sit deeper into the left kua. Your weight is sinking. You are "loading" the left leg, compressing it in a way that will allow for an explosive burst of power if needed. The Dantien rotates down the left side.

Image 9-D – The fingers curl and point to the right as you sit deeper into the left kua.

As you sit deeper into the left kua, your waist turns a little to the left (Image 9-D) and your fingers curl to the point that they are pointing to the right. You are now ready to pick up the ground from the left foot into the right hand.

Image 9-E – Push the ground from the left foot through the right hand as the arm uncoils and the hand pushes to the right.

Connecting the ground from the left foot to the right hand, relax the right kua and begin shifting your weight to the right as your arm uncoils and your palm spears to the right (Image 9-E). Your Dantien is rotating to the right.

Image 9-F – The hand stabs out to the right as you close into the right kua.

As you see in Image 9-F, you push the hand to the right until the arm uncoils, as you sit into the right kua and have turned the Dantien to the right. Next, you will spiral the hand as you raise the body.

Image 9-G – Raise the body and spiral the hand so that the palm is up and you are back in the starting posture.

Let the body rise as your hand uncoils until the palm faces up again and you are back in the original position (Image 9-G). You can continue the exercise as many times as you want, smoothing it out and working on the body mechanics.

The Diving Palm Spiral is deceptive in its application for self-defense. Inside this exercise are deflections, bumps, groin strikes, spearhand strikes, and takedowns.

Sometimes, I will work on one of the Silk-Reeling exercises, such as this one, and focus on different mechanics. I will do it a few times and focus on whole-body movement, making sure all parts are moving. Another time, I will focus on how I am relaxing, opening and closing the kua. Another time, I will focus on maintaining the ground path and peng jin.

The purpose of all this practice, of course, is to take the body mechanics you are developing and apply them to your forms. Then, you apply them to self-defense. It is a step-by-step progression that requires a different mindset than some martial arts, and usually more time, because we have to unlearn bad habits from a lifetime of moving in a different way, with tense muscles and stiff joints.

Silk-Reeling Exercise 10 – Single Elbow Spiral

One of my favorite techniques in close-up fighting is a concept that Bruce Lee was fond of saying.

"Be water, my friend," he would say.

By being like water, I flow around obstacles that my opponent puts in my way. Like water, I find a way around his defenses and I strike. I "listen" to his changing force as I touch him, and often, when he tries to block my strike, I flow around his defense with an elbow to the face. Like water, I find my way in.

This exercise will help you learn how. It appears to be a wrist-spiraling exercise, but its main purpose is to spiral the elbow. The wrist spiraling is a bonus.

Although this is primarily an elbow-spiraling exercise, the entire body should be working with the movement.

Image 10-A – Starting in a random position at the top of the circle, with the knuckles of the right hand pressed lightly onto my ribs.

You can start with your hand in any position. I put the knuckles against the ribs (Image 10-A). The hand is not closed into a fist. You will see why in the next image. Remember to relax through the arm.

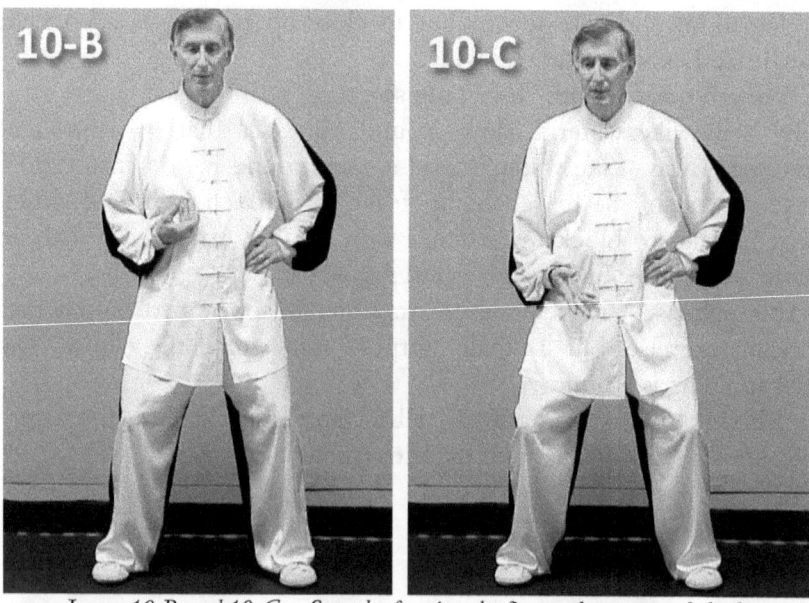

Image 10-B and 10-C – Start by fanning the fingers down toward the kua. This causes your elbow to move slightly backward.

In Image 10-B, you start fanning the fingers downward. In doing that, the elbow rotates down. You begin sitting into the kua, sinking the energy and compressing into the right leg. The Dantien is rotating forward and down, in the same direction as the fingers.

In Image 10-C, continue fanning the fingers toward the kua. The elbow will go back and down a little more and the downward energy of the body is still compressing the right leg.

Image 10-D and 10-E – The elbow begins rising as the fingers circle toward the back, and as the knuckles circle down the torso, the elbow spirals up and forward.

Next, as the fingers fan downward and prepare to make a circle to the back, the elbow begins circling up (Image 10-D). The ground is now clearly connected from the right foot into the right elbow, and your back is beginning to bow out as the Dantien reaches the bottom of the circle and prepares to go "up the back."

The fingers continue making a circle, pointing behind you as the elbow spirals over the top and forward (Image 10-E). At the top of the circle, the left leg picks up the ground path. The lower back is starting to unbow as the Dantien rotation reaches the top of its circle up the back.

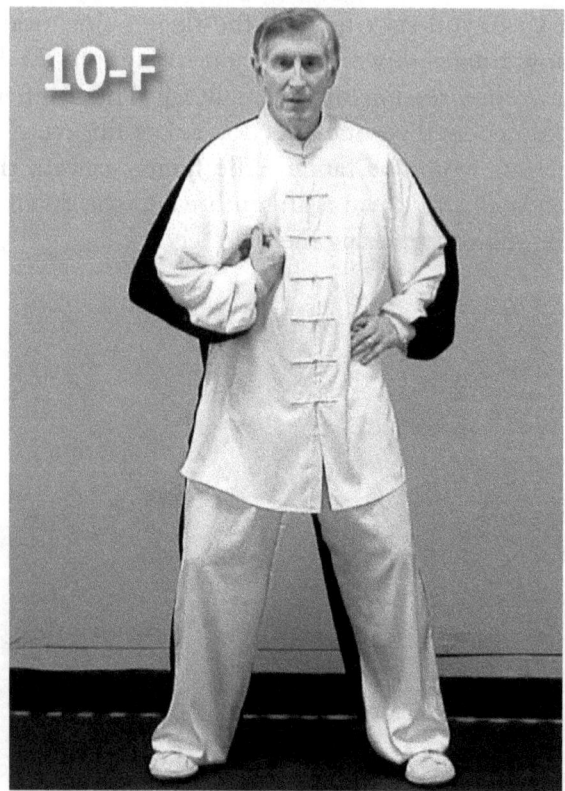

Image 10-F – The elbow spirals over and downward.

The elbow continues its rotation over and down the front, as the fingers begin to fan out down the torso again. The Dantien is rotating forward and down. The ground from the left foot connects with the elbow as it goes over the top and downward. When it reaches the bottom, the ground shifts to the right foot. You are sinking again into the kua as the elbow rotates downward.

Do this exercise as many times as you want, then reverse it and do the rotation the opposite way. See the images that start on the next page.

Reversing the Direction of Single Elbow Spiral

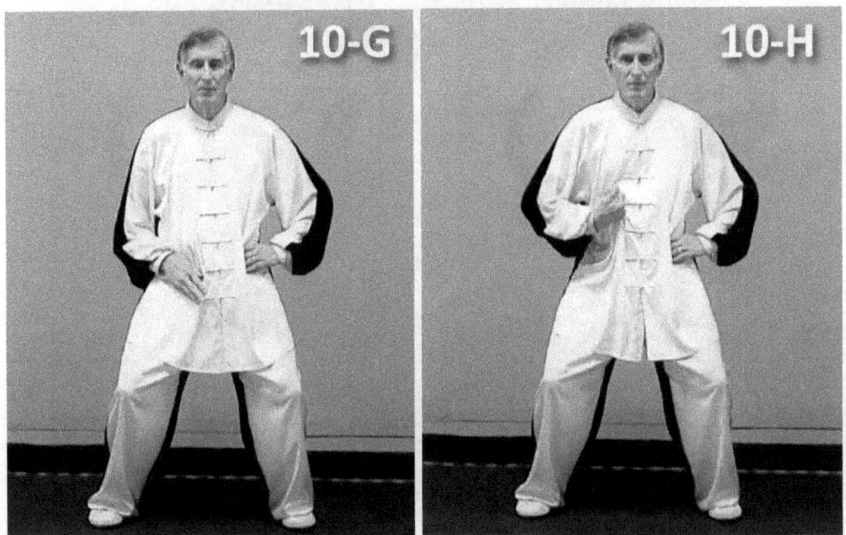

Image 10-G – Doing the reverse direction, starting with the fingers fanned out at the kua. 10-H – Moving the fingertips toward the armpit to begin the circle.

To do the Single Elbow Spiral in the opposite direction, begin with the fingers fanned out at the kua (Image 10-G) and the energy sunk. I am closed into the kua. Naturally, you can begin anywhere in the spiral, but I am choosing this posture.

As shown in Image 10-H, I begin by spiraling the wrist and bringing my fingers toward my right armpit. The ground is connected from the right foot into the hand as it rises. The Dantien is rotating up the front and the Dantien area bows out (convex) while the lower back unbows (concave).

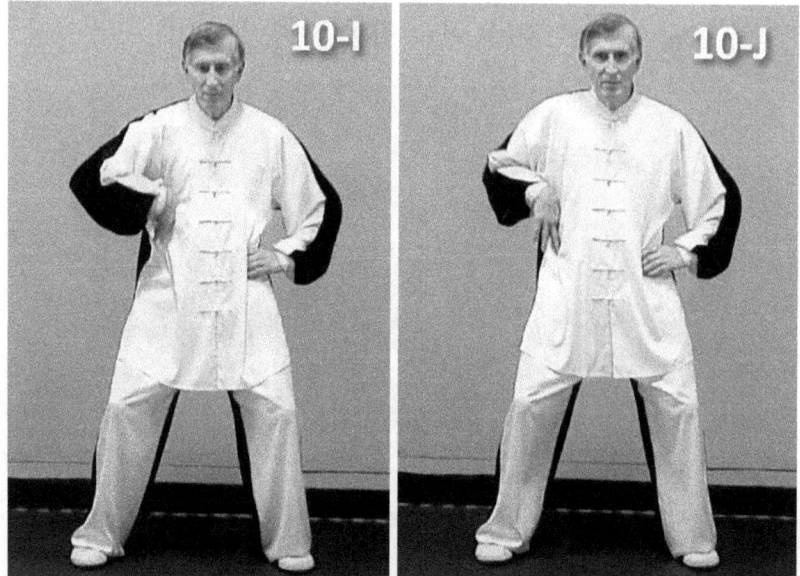

*Image 10-I – The elbow spirals up as the hand prepares to spiral down.
Image 10-J – Fan the fingers out as the elbow rotates downward (behind you).*

The ground from the left foot now connects to the right elbow as it rises and begins to circle over and back. The fingers in Image 10-I are pointed behind me and are preparing to continue the rotation downward. I have opened the kua. As the wrist and hand rotate, so does the Dantien. The lower back is beginning to fill up.

Your lower back bows out (convex) as the elbow descends and the fingers fan out in their rotation (Image 10-J). You are starting to sink into the kua and dropping your energy, the compression building in your right leg.

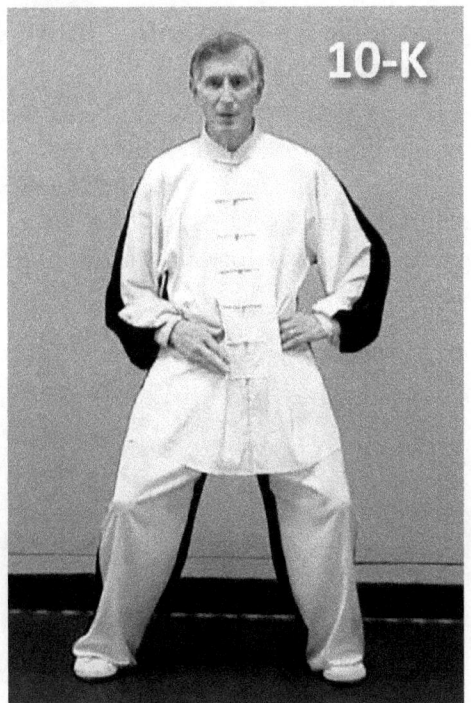

Image 10-K – Back to the original position, ready to keep going into the next one.

Finally, you return to the original position. From here, you can continue doing the reverse spiral, or change directions again.

After doing the right arm as many times as you want, it is time to do the same exercise with the left. Do both sides an equal number of times, forward and backward.

Silk-Reeling Exercise 11 – Double Elbow Spiral

The Double Elbow Spiral is done the same way as the Single Elbow Spiral, but it is done with both elbows simultaneously (hence, the name; clever, isn't it?). Just like the Single Elbow Spiral, this should be done in both directions.

The next sequence shows the forward direction. Remember to relax through both arms.

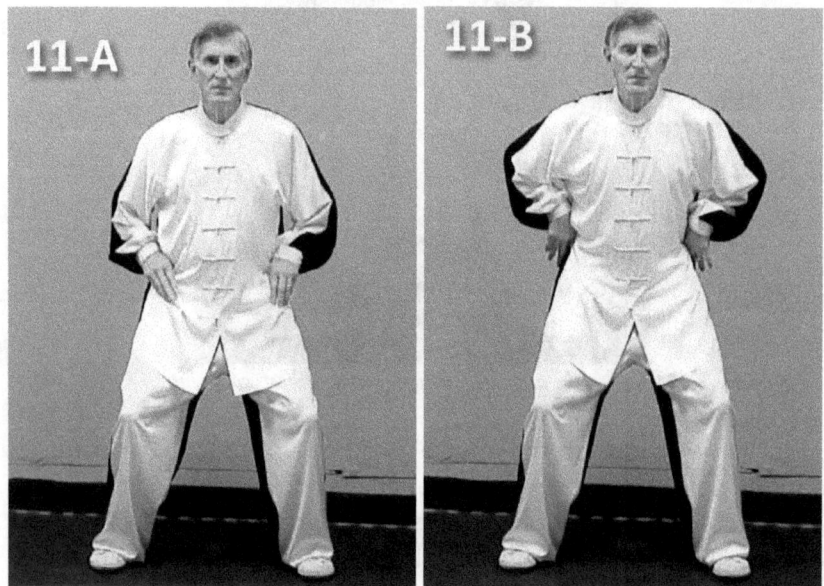

Image 11-A – Start with both hands at the kua.
Image 11-B – Point the fingers behind you as the rotation begins. The elbows go back a little more and begin rising as the lower back fills up (convex).

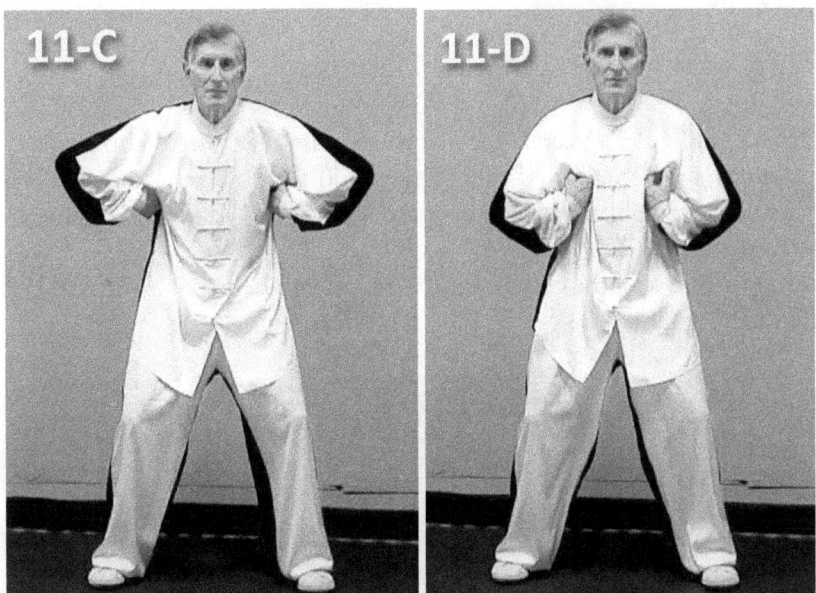

Image 11-C – Wrists and fingers continue rotating and lower back begins to unbow as the Dantien rotates up the back and the elbows reach the top of their rotation.

Image 11-D – The elbows rotate forward and down. The fingers reach the top of their rotation and so does the Dantien.

Image 11-E – Fingers start to fan forward, elbows drop and begin going back.

Image 11-F – Fingers fan to the kua and sink your energy; relax into the kua.

Using Elbow Spiral in Self-Defense

Every silk-reeling exercise, since they contain all six key body mechanics, are actually self-defense techniques. As I mentioned earlier, several fighting applications are embedded into each of the exercises.

Here is one way the Single Elbow Spiral can be used in self-defense.

Image S-1 – Justin punches at me at close range.

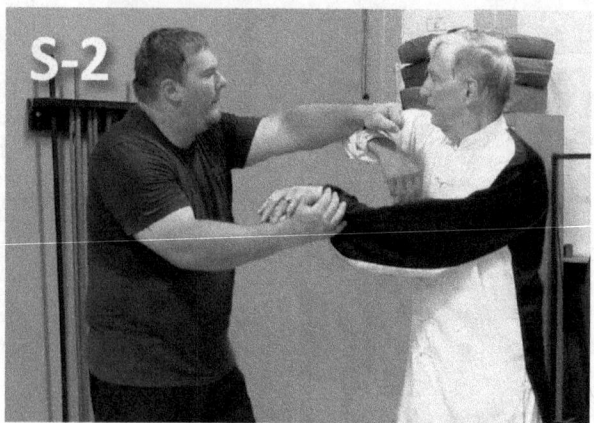

Image S-2 – I start spiraling my elbow over his punching arm.

As you can see in the two pictures above, at close-up fighting range, you try to stick to your opponent, and when you feel him throwing a punch, you deflect it with your forearm as you spiral the elbow over. Image S-3 below shows the final result of this technique.

Image S-3 – My elbow has spiraled over to strike him in the face while his punch has been deflected by my forearm. It misses.

Silk-Reeling Exercise 12 – Ankle Circles

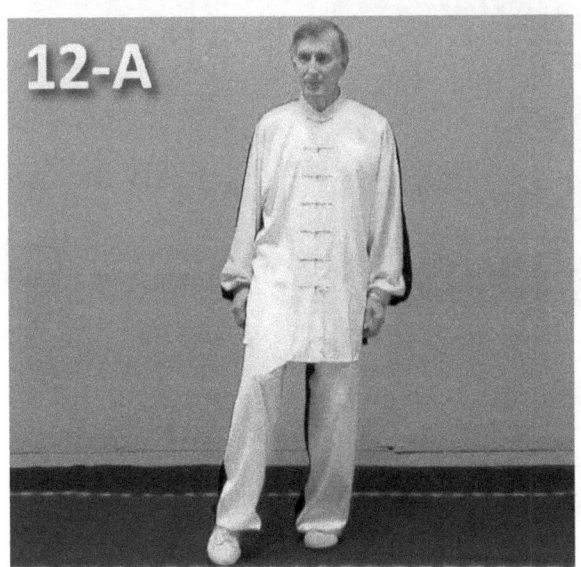

Image 12-A – Put your weight on the left foot and raise the right heel.

Begin by putting your weight on one leg and raising the other heel. In this example, I'll start by raising the right heel. It is common for some people, when they put their weight onto one leg, to stick the hip out to help balance. Try to avoid that. Notice in Image 12-A, the outside edge of my left hip is basically in line with the outer edge of my left foot. Raise the right heel and relax. Sink your energy.

The heel will make a clockwise circle (if you are looking down at the foot), going right to left.

One of your goals in this exercise is to develop a connected feeling throughout your leg to the foot. You want to feel the spiral from the Dantien through the ankle and heel, like a connected wave through the leg. The kua opens and closes with the circling of the heel.

The foot that is circling remains very lightly on the toe. Virtually no weight is put on the toe; almost 100% of your weight is on the supporting leg.

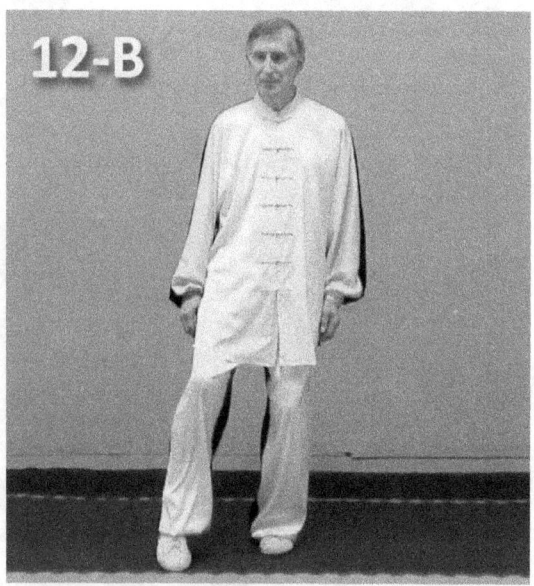

Image 12-B – Keeping on the toe of the right foot, circle the heel to the right as you open the right kua.

Open the right kua as you begin circling the heel to the right. The Dantien is also circling to the right. It will make a horizontal circle.

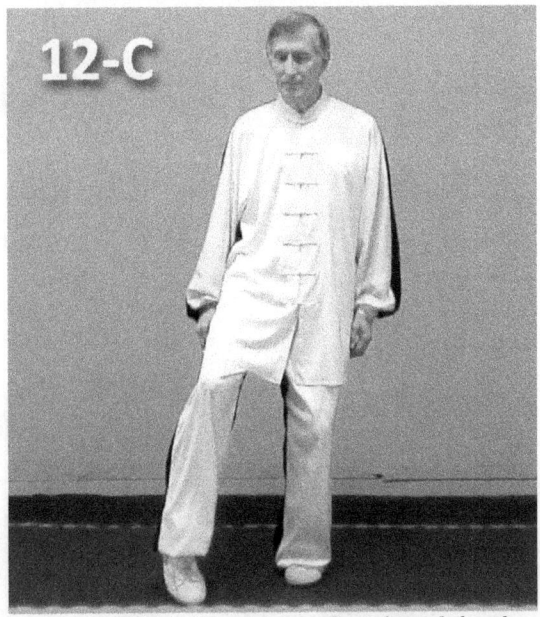

Image 12-C – The heel continues to the right and then forward.

The heel continues circling to the right and forward, opening the right kua a little more (Image 12-C). The Dantien is also circling toward the front on the right side. Remain very relaxed in the right kua.

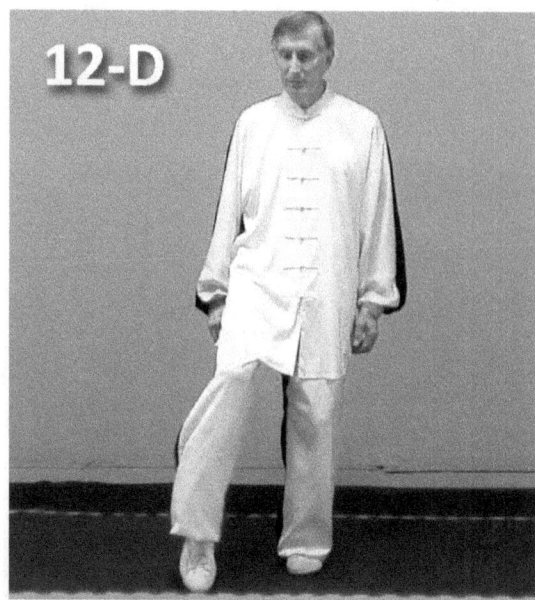

Image 12-D --

In Image 12-D, the heel circles forward and the right kua begins to close a little.

In the next photo, Image 12-E, the heel circles to the left. The Dantien is also rotating to the left.

Image 12-E – The heel circles to the left.

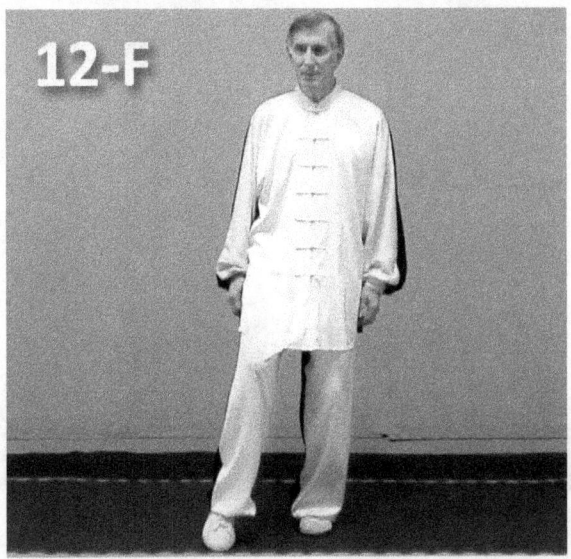

Image 12-F – The heel returns to its original starting position.

Continue doing circles in the same direction, then reverse directions. After practicing long enough with the right foot, switch and do the same spiral exercise with the left foot.

Silk-Reeling Exercise 13 – Leg Spirals

The final silk-reeling exercise in this book is an excellent method of developing your kua and spiraling through the legs, but also is tremendously helpful for developing the stabilizer muscles in your legs, which in turn improves your balance.

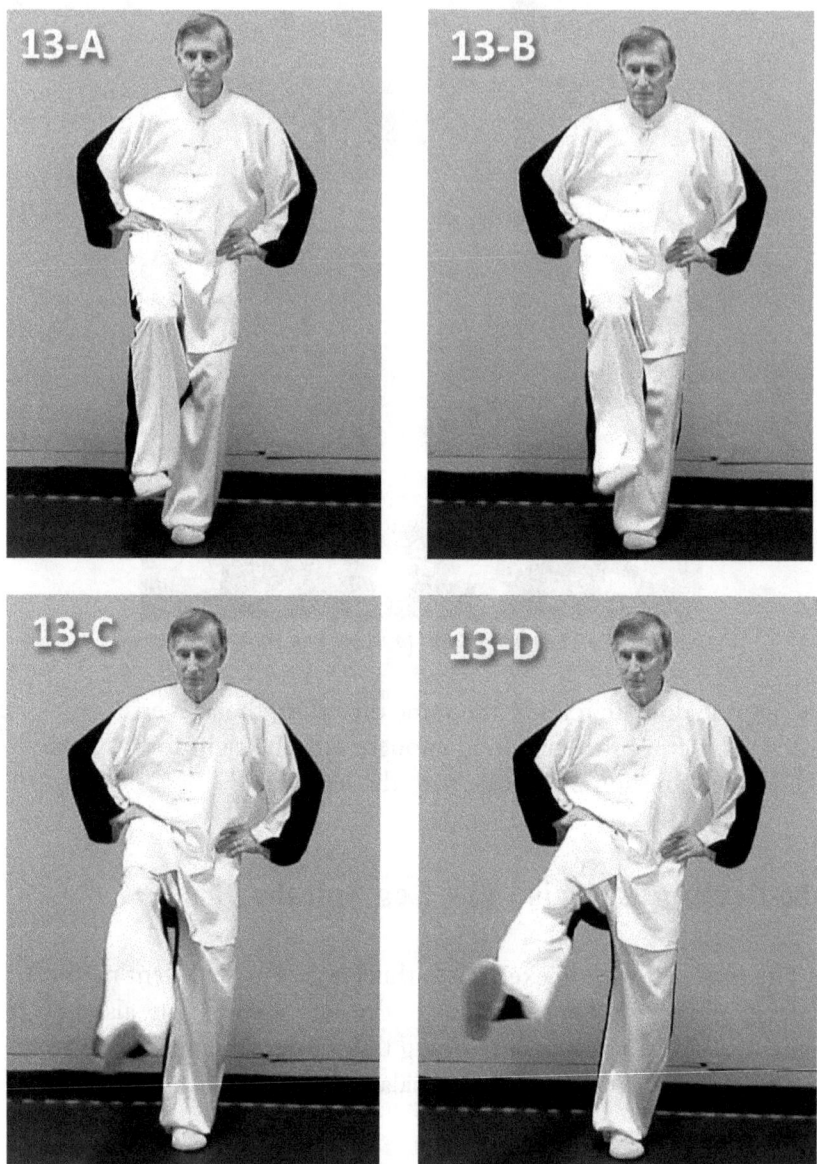

Lift the right leg and close the kua (Image 13-A). Begin spiraling through the foot, angling the bottom of your foot out slightly as you close the kua even more (Image 13-B). Image 13-C shows the leg beginning to circle to the right. The kua begins to open. Image 13-D shows the circle continuing and the spiraling through the leg extends through the edge of the foot, with the kua continuing to open.

 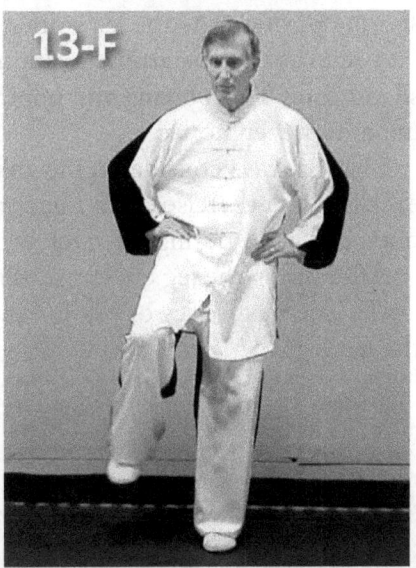

In Image 13-E, the edge of the foot is at the side. And the circle continues through Images 13-F and 13-G, where you return to the starting position.

As you do this exercise, rotate the Dantien in a horizontal circle to the right, then it circles across the lower back as the kick returns to starting position. As the leg spirals out, the lower back unbows; as the kick returns to the starting position, the lower back fills up and bows slightly out. This bowing and unbowing is subtle. The untrained eye might not even notice.

I have always considered the ankle circles and leg circles to be excellent kua exercises, and I generally focus on relaxing the kua as I open and close during the circles.

After doing the leg circle a dozen or two dozen times, reverse the circle. The next series of photos shows a reversal of direction using the left leg.

 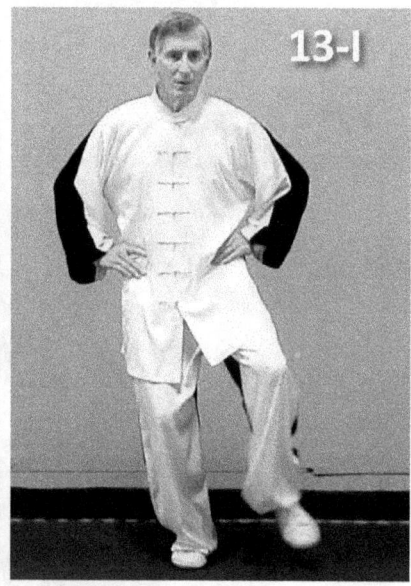

In Image 13-H, I pick up the left foot and close the kua. Image 13-I shows the counter-clockwise circle beginning, with the left kua opening and the Dantien rotating to the left.

The images on the next page, 13-J through 13-M, show the completion of the circle. It goes out to the left, forward, then continues the circle to the right and then back again. The Dantien is rotating in the same direction the foot is traveling, and in Images 13-K through 13-M, the left kua is closing. The lower back unbows as the leg goes out, and fills up as the leg goes inward.

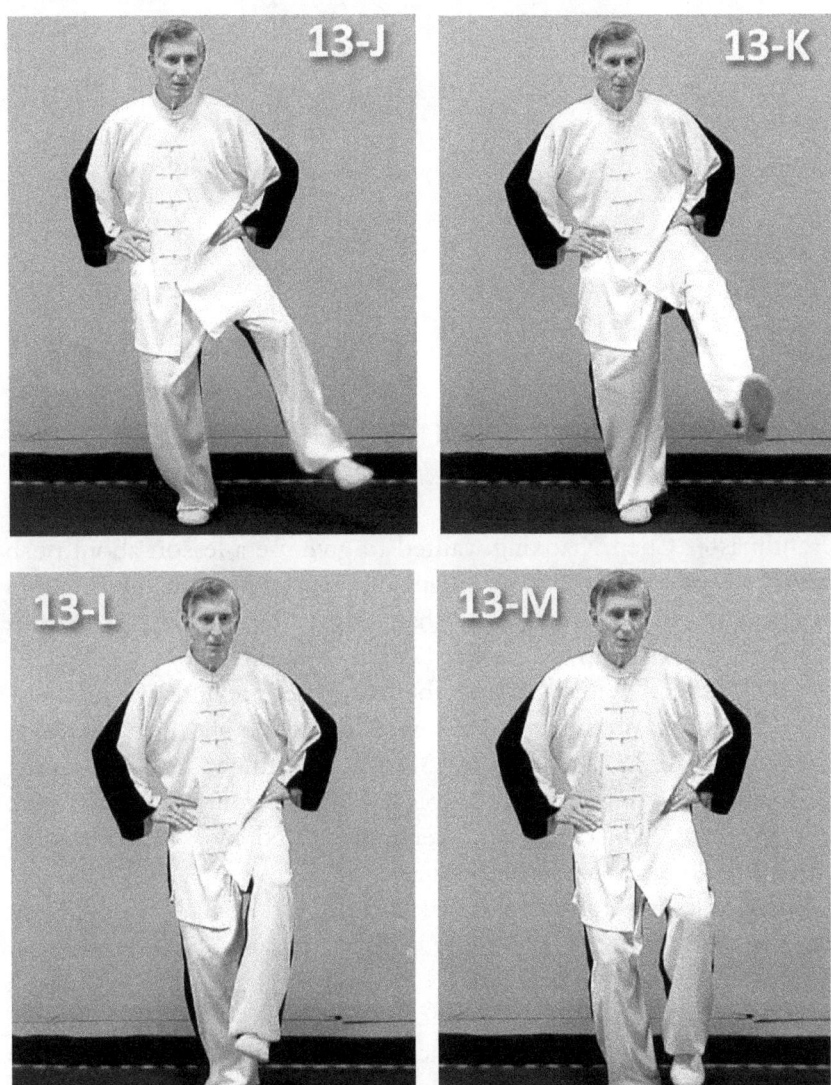

As always, you want to connect the ground from the supporting leg through the circling foot. Whole-body connection is always important. You never simply move one part of the body. This means the right foot will connect with the Dantien, which connects with the left leg and foot.

8 WHERE DO YOU GO FROM HERE?

Grandmaster Chen Xiaoxing wanted to give me a lesson about push hands, so we went to my basement. He was staying in my home in Moline, Illinois for a week as a "thank you" because I sponsored his visa to do a workshop tour in the United States in 2006.

I had trained with Xiaoxing before. The previous year, I was invited to spend a couple of days with him alone with my teacher at that time, Mark Wasson, in Mark's apartment in Livermore, California. It was a great couple of days, going through each movement of Laojia Yilu and being corrected by Chen Xiaoxing, with Mark doing a bit of interpreting.

Chen Xiaoxing could not speak a word of English. I could not speak a word of Mandarin. Before he arrived at my home, a year after the private lessons in California, I studied language CDs so I could say a few phrases to him. It did not work. When I spoke to him, he was mystified. So we communicated when we did push hands through physical demonstrations.

In the basement, we touched hands and started into a push hands pattern that involved taking a step toward your opponent while maintaining contact. He took a step at me. We did the pattern, our hands and arms in contact, circling and circling, then I took a step toward him.

Wham!

Chen Xiaoxing had put me on the carpet. On my back. And I had no idea how he had done it.

Surprised, I stood up and we touched hands again. We went

through the pattern, our arms circling, and I took another step toward him.

Wham? I was on my back again.

I laughed. Xiaoxing laughed.

Then it happened again, and then again, and I came to see my carpet, and my basement ceiling, from an entirely new perspective.

We both continued to laugh each time it happened. He must have been thinking, "This white dude is a SLOW learner."

I was on my back more often that evening than a New York City ho. I have to admit it took me about ten times being thrown onto the carpet before I understood what he was doing.

Without me realizing it, he was breaking my structure, taking control of my center, and taking advantage of it to put me on the ground. It seemed so effortless, I could not for the longest time figure out how he was doing it, but it was one of the most important lessons I have learned about using the real principles of Tai Chi.

That is Grandmaster Chen Xiaoxing putting me on the floor in 2006.

It took 10 years of practicing and thinking and experimenting and thinking harder to take that insight deeper. I was distracted a bit by some minor events: losing a lung, living in heart failure for a couple of years, coughing up blood, sudden trips to the Intensive Care Unit, that sort of thing. You know, the type of thing we all go through.

But I kept pushing, and over time, the lesson Chen Xiaoxing taught me in my basement developed a strong root of its own. It gave me insights into how the "energies" and methods of Tai Chi are used in close-up self-defense. Without saying a word, he taught me the deepest "secret" I had learned about how to use Tai Chi in a fight.

You see, the concepts in this book are just the beginning. On your martial arts journey, this book is the signpost that says, "Start here."

You work on these mechanics as you practice Silk-Reeling Exercises, forms and fighting techniques. You take them further when practicing push hands, one-steps, light sparring, contact sparring and grappling. You begin with concepts and forms, proceed to push hands and applications, continue to working with partners, and finally, you develop the sensitivity skills, the "listening" skills, and the connection skills so that you know when your partner is going to move almost before he does. You feel his force, you neutralize it, you break his structure, control his center and take him down without muscular force, by putting him off-balance, breaking his structure, and controlling his center.

That is where you go from here. It should not take a lifetime to become skilled at the internal arts. But what it will take is hard work, thoughtful study and feedback. It will take good instruction.

We all have a visual image of ourselves as Bruce Lee or Chen

Xiaowang when we are doing martial arts. But if we do not have feedback, we usually look like Laurel and Hardy.

It takes a special personality to persist in the internal arts. If you are lucky, and you have a teacher who picks you apart, and tells you what you are doing wrong, you have the opportunity to develop skill. But if your ego is fragile, and you cannot handle criticism, you will never achieve high-level skill.

Feedback is crucial to improve your skill in the internal arts. That is why members of my website are able to set up 15-to-20-minute live Facetime or Skype video chats with me on a regular basis as part of their membership. They demonstrate movements and I coach them to make them better. It works.

My goal has always been to cut your development time. No one should have to waste years, and thousands of dollars, learning from instructors who are charismatic but are teaching empty arts, or they are teaching quality arts but do not know how to teach their students, or they parcel out information bit by bit, very slowly, to keep your money rolling in. I do not believe in that.

That is why I wrote this book.

For decades, I have seen a list of the "10 Most Important Tips for Tai Chi," and it includes advice such as "lift your head as if it is being suspended in air", and "keep your chest depressed and your back raised." You can find similar tips for Xingyi and Bagua practice.

These might be tips to focus on later in your practice, but if you are not grounded, if you do not maintain peng, and if you do not follow the other body mechanics in this book, it does not matter whether you lift your head or depress your chest or raise your back.

And it does not matter how well you can hold a posture if, as soon as you begin moving there are breaks in your mechanics. It does not matter how long you can hold up a kick or how low you can go in your stance. It does not matter how pretty your form looks to the untrained eye. If you have no internal strength, the rest is pointless.

Mental and Physical Balance

"Internal strength" is not the only important concept I try to get across in my teaching. The word "connect" is an important concept, not just for the whole-body connection that you develop physically, but also for the way you connect with other people and the world.

Two of the top goals of an internal artist are to maintain your physical balance and your mental balance. We attempt to remain "centered" at all times. In life, we are faced constantly with people and events that attempt to put us off-balance. We try to connect with these people and remain centered through the ups and downs of life.

Through the practice of the internal arts of Chinese gongfu we learn to maintain our physical balance, and in the practice of our philosophy we can achieve the goal of mental balance. We can "connect" with others, even someone who is trying to attack us. We can find our balance again when life pulls the rug out from under us. When we do this, "internal strength" takes on a deeper meaning.

This book is about the body mechanics required for physical balance and relaxed power. I discuss some of the philosophy for mental balance on my blog: www.internalfightingartsblog.com. I invite you to drop by and say hello. And feel free to reach out and say hello by email or chat with me on Facebook. My page is at www.facebook.com/InternalFightingArts. If you are ever passing through the Quad Cities, on I-80 at the border of Iowa and Illinois, let me know and drop by. Maybe we'll practice for an hour or two. We can go over some of these internal body mechanics in person.

Thank you for buying this book. I wish you the best of luck in your martial arts journey.

Ken Gullette
July, 2018

ABOUT THE AUTHOR

Ken Gullette was born on January 24, 1953. He started his martial arts journey on September 20, 1973, in his hometown of Lexington, Kentucky. Less than two years later, he graduated from Eastern Kentucky University with a double major in journalism and broadcasting, and began an award-winning 22-year career in radio and TV news. One of Ken's jobs was producer at WLWT in Cincinnati, where he worked with Jerry Springer. In 1987, while working as a news producer in Omaha, he discovered the internal arts. In 1998, after starting his second career in public relations and media relations, he discovered Chen Tai Chi, and that changed everything. Ken has learned from some top Chen family masters and their students. He has nearly 30 DVDs on the market, available on Amazon and through his websites, and his online "school" has members around the world who pay a monthly fee to study nearly 1,000 video lessons and downloadable pdf documents and e-books. His podcast, "Internal Fighting Arts," features interviews with internal arts teachers from around the world. He has been blogging since 2006 at InternalFightingArtsBlog.com. He is a tournament champion and began teaching the internal arts in 1997. Ken is ecstatically married to Nancy. They live in Moline, Illinois (part of the Quad Cities) and between the two of them, they have three grown children and six grandchildren, who all consider Ken a little bit goofy. He loves Bruce Lee, the Marx Brothers, Laurel and Hardy, "Airplane," "Young Frankenstein," making people laugh, including his wife (as long as she doesn't *POINT* and laugh), and he loves philosophical Taoism and Zen. Ken's daily goal is to "remain centered at all times."

You've Read the Book!
Now Get the Instruction on VIDEO!
Bring this Book's Lessons to *Life*!
www.InternalBodyMechanics.com

What You Get:
Dozens of Streaming Video Lessons Covering:
** Ground Path exercises
** Peng Jin
** Whole-Body Movement
** Silk-Reeling exercises
** Opening/Closing the Kua
** Dantien Rotation
** PDF Downloads
A One-Time Payment – No Recurring Payments
Plus Two Bonuses Mailed To You:
Ken's "Internal Strength" DVD (mailed to you)
Ken's "Silk-Reeling Energy" DVD (mailed to you)

Try TWO WEEKS FREE on Ken's Website
www.InternalFightingArts.com

--Information That Will Cut Years Off Your Training Time and Save Thousands of Dollars n Lesson Fees--

--Nearly 1,000 Video Lessons Streaming 24/7--

--Step-by-Step Instruction in Internal Strength, Taiji, Xingy, Bagua, Qigong – Forms, Weapons & Self-Defense--

--You Get It All Now! No Waiting for Lessons--

--An Emphasis on Internal Body Mechanics--

--Live Video Coaching with Ken at No Extra Cost--

--No Contracts and Cancel Anytime--

--PDF documents and eBooks at no extra cost--

Go Deeper with Ken's Instructional DVDs
Internal Strength – Silk-Reeling – Taiji
Xingyi – Bagua – Qigong

Three Places to Buy Ken's DVDs:

Amazon.com -- (Prime shipping available)

www.Kungfu4u.com -- Free shipping worldwide plus Buy 2 Get 1 DVD Free

www.InternalFightingArtsBlog.com – Free shipping worldwide plus Buy 2 Get 1 DVD Free

Listen to Ken's **"Internal Fighting Arts" Podcast**
on iTunes, Stitcher, Podbean & other Distributors

Philosophy, News and Internal Arts Techniques on
Ken's Blog:
www.InternalFightingArtsBlog.com

Ken's Internal Arts Facebook Page:
www.Facebook.com/InternalFightingArts

www.ingramcontent.com/pod-product-compliance
Lightning Source LLC
Chambersburg PA
CBHW050634160426
43194CB00010B/1665